Local Governance in Timor-Leste

Across many parts of the postcolonial world, it is everyday reality for people to cross regularly between state-based and customary governance, institutions and norms. This book examines this phenomenon in the context of the villages of Timor-Leste, and the state-building efforts that have been conducted by the Timorese government and international development agencies since the vote for independence in 1999.

Drawing on five years of ethnographic fieldwork in the remote, rural areas of Timor-Leste, the book provides a critical analysis of the challenges that communities face when navigating co-existing customary and state-based structures and norms in a context where customary law continues to be the central guiding force. It also explores the various creative ways in which local leaders and community members make sense of their local governance environment. It then draws on these insights to provide a more nuanced, contextualised account of the impact of institutional interventions, state-building and democratisation within these villages. While set in the context of state- and nation-building efforts following Timor-Leste's vote for independence, the book also provides a broader examination of the issues that arise for the postcolonial state in adequately meeting the needs of its citizens. Further, it explores the challenges that are met by communities when incorporating state influences and demands into their everyday lives. Expanding the scope of empirical Timor-Leste scholarship by moving beyond anthropological description and providing the first detailed political analysis of local-level governance in contemporary Timorese communities, this book is a valuable contribution to studies on Asian Politics, Governance and International Studies.

Deborah Cummins is an academic, consultant and trainer on issues of postcolonial local governance, and international and community development. She is the founder of Bridging Peoples, www.bridgingpeoples.com.

Routledge Contemporary Southeast Asia Series

1 **Land Tenure, Conservation and Development in Southeast Asia**
Peter Eaton

2 **The Politics of Indonesia-Malaysia Relations**
One kin, two nations
Joseph Chinyong Liow

3 **Governance and Civil Society in Myanmar**
Education, health and environment
Helen James

4 **Regionalism in Post-Suharto Indonesia**
Edited by Maribeth Erb, Priyambudi Sulistiyanto and Carole Faucher

5 **Living with Transition in Laos**
Market integration in Southeast Asia
Jonathan Rigg

6 **Christianity, Islam and Nationalism in Indonesia**
Charles E. Farhadian

7 **Violent Conflicts in Indonesia**
Analysis, representation, resolution
Edited by Charles A. Coppel

8 **Revolution, Reform and Regionalism in Southeast Asia**
Cambodia, Laos and Vietnam
Ronald Bruce St John

9 **The Politics of Tyranny in Singapore and Burma**
Aristotle and the rhetoric of benevolent despotism
Stephen McCarthy

10 **Ageing in Singapore**
Service needs and the state
Peggy Teo, Kalyani Mehta, Leng Leng Thang and Angelique Chan

11 **Security and Sustainable Development in Myanmar**
Helen James

12 **Expressions of Cambodia**
The politics of tradition, identity and change
Edited by Leakthina Chau-Pech Ollier and Tim Winter

13 **Financial Fragility and Instability in Indonesia**
Yasuyuki Matsumoto

14 **The Revival of Tradition in Indonesian Politics**
The deployment of *adat* from colonialism to indigenism
Edited by Jamie S. Davidson and David Henley

15 **Communal Violence and Democratization in Indonesia**
Small town wars
Gerry van Klinken

16 **Singapore in the Global System**
Relationship, structure and change
Peter Preston

17 **Chinese Big Business in Indonesia**
The state of the Capital
Christian Chua

18 **Ethno-religious Violence in Indonesia**
From soil to God
Chris Wilson

19 **Ethnic Politics in Burma**
States of conflict
Ashley South

20 **Democratization in Post-Suharto Indonesia**
Edited by Marco Bünte and Andreas Ufen

21 **Party Politics and Democratization in Indonesia**
Golkar in the Post-Suharto era
Dirk Tomsa

22 **Community, Environment and Local Governance in Indonesia**
Locating the Commonweal
Edited by Carol Warren and John F. McCarthy

23 **Rebellion and Reform in Indonesia**
Jakarta's security and autonomy policies in Aceh
Michelle Ann Miller

24 **Hadrami Arabs in Present-day Indonesia**
An Indonesia-oriented Group with an Arab Signature
Frode F. Jacobsen

25 **Vietnam's Political Process**
How education shapes political decision making
Casey Lucius

26 **Muslims in Singapore**
Piety, politics and policies
Kamaludeen Mohamed Nasir, Alexius A. Pereira and Bryan S. Turner

27 **Timor Leste**
Politics, history and culture
Andrea Katalin Molnar

28 **Gender and Transitional Justice**
The women of East Timor
Susan Harris Rimmer

29 **Environmental Cooperation in Southeast Asia**
ASEAN's regime for transboundary haze pollution
Paruedee Nguitragool

30 **The Theatre and the State in Singapore**
Terence Chong

31 **Ending Forced Labour in Myanmar**
Engaging a pariah regime
Richard Horsey

32 **Security, Development and Nation-Building in Timor-Leste**
A cross-sectoral assessment
Edited by Vandra Harris and Andrew Goldsmith

33 **The Politics of Religion in Indonesia**
Syncretism, orthodoxy, and religious contention in Java and Bali
Edited by Michel Picard and Remy Madinier

34 **Singapore's Ageing Population**
Managing healthcare and end of life decisions
Edited by Wing-Cheong Chan

35 **Changing Marriage Patterns in Southeast Asia**
Economic and socio-cultural dimensions
Edited by Gavin W. Jones, Terence H. Hull and Maznah Mohamad

36 **The Political Resurgence of the Military in Southeast Asia**
Conflict and leadership
Edited by Marcus Mietzner

37 **Neoliberal Morality in Singapore**
How family policies make state and society
Youyenn Teo

38 **Local Politics in Indonesia**
Pathways to power
Nankyung Choi

39 **Separatist Conflict in Indonesia**
The long-distance politics of the Acehnese diaspora
Antje Missbach

40 **Corruption and Law in Indonesia**
The unravelling of Indonesia's anti-corruption framework through law and legal process
Simon Butt

41 **Men and Masculinities in Southeast Asia**
Edited by Michele Ford and Lenore Lyons

42 **Justice and Governance in East Timor**
Indigenous approaches and the 'New Subsistence State'
Rod Nixon

43 **Population Policy and Reproduction in Singapore**
Making future citizens
Shirley Hsiao-Li Sun

44 **Labour Migration and Human Trafficking in Southeast Asia**
Critical perspectives
Michele Ford, Lenore Lyons and Willem van Schendel

45 **Singapore Malays**
Being ethnic minority and Muslim in a global city-state
Hussin Mutalib

46 **Political Change and Territoriality in Indonesia**
Provincial proliferation
Ehito Kimura

47 **Southeast Asia and the Cold War**
Edited by Albert Lau

48 **Legal Pluralism in Indonesia**
Bridging the unbridgeable
Ratno Lukito

49 **Building a People-Oriented Security Community the ASEAN way**
Alan Collins

50 **Parties and Parliaments in Southeast Asia**
Non-partisan chambers in Indonesia, the Philippines and Thailand
Roland Rich

51 **Social Activism in Southeast Asia**
Edited by Michele Ford

52 **Chinese Indonesians Reassessed**
History, religion and belonging
Edited by Siew-Min Sai and Chang-Yau Hoon

53 **Journalism and Conflict in Indonesia**
From reporting violence to promoting peace
Steve Sharp

54 **The Technological State in Indonesia**
The co-constitution of high technology and authoritarian politics
Sulfikar Amir

55 **Party Politics in Southeast Asia**
Clientelism and electoral competition in Indonesia, Thailand and the Philippines
Edited by Dirk Tomsa and Andreas Ufen

56 **Culture, Religion and Conflict in Muslim Southeast Asia**
Negotiating tense pluralisms
Edited by Joseph Camilleri and Sven Schottmann

57 **Global Indonesia**
Jean Gelman Taylor

58 **Cambodia and the Politics of Aesthetics**
Alvin Cheng-Hin Lim

59 **Adolescents in Contemporary Indonesia**
Lyn Parker and Pam Nilan

60 **Development and the Environment in East Timor**
Authority, participation and equity
Christopher Shepherd

61 **Law and Religion in Indonesia**
Faith, conflict and the courts
Melissa Crouch

62 **Islam in Modern Thailand**
Faith, philanthropy and politics
Rajeswary Ampalavanar Brown

63 **New Media and the Nation in Malaysia**
Malaysianet
Susan Leong

64 **Human Trafficking in Cambodia**
Chendo Keo

65 **Islam, Politics and Youth in Malaysia**
The pop-Islamist reinvention of PAS
Dominik Mueller

66 **The Future of Singapore**
Population, society and the nature of the state
Kamaludeen Mohamed Nasir and Bryan S. Turner

67 **Southeast Asia and the European Union**
Non-traditional security crises and cooperation
Naila Maier-Knapp

68 **Rhetoric, Violence, and the Decolonization of East Timor**
David Hicks

69 **Local Governance in Timor-Leste**
Lessons in postcolonial state-building
Deborah Cummins

70 **Media Consumption in Malaysia**
A Hermeneutics of human behaviour
Tony Wilson

71 **Philippine Politics**
Progress and problems in a localist democracy
Lynn T. White III

Local Governance in Timor-Leste
Lessons in postcolonial state-building

Deborah Cummins

LONDON AND NEW YORK

First published 2015
by Routledge
2 Park Square, Milton Park, Abingdon, Oxon OX14 4RN

and by Routledge
711 Third Avenue, New York, NY 10017

First issued in paperback 2017

Routledge is an imprint of the Taylor & Francis Group, an informa business

© 2015 Deborah Cummins

The right of Deborah Cummins to be identified as author of this work has been asserted by her in accordance with sections 77 and 78 of the Copyright, Designs and Patents Act 1988.

All rights reserved. No part of this book may be reprinted or reproduced or utilised in any form or by any electronic, mechanical, or other means, now known or hereafter invented, including photocopying and recording, or in any information storage or retrieval system, without permission in writing from the publishers.

Trademark notice: Product or corporate names may be trademarks or registered trademarks, and are used only for identification and explanation without intent to infringe.

British Library Cataloguing in Publication Data
A catalogue record for this book is available from the British Library

Library of Congress Cataloguing in Publication data
Cummins, Deborah (Writer on Timor-Leste) author.
　Local governance in Timor-Leste : lessons in postcolonial state-building / Deborah Cummins.
　　pages　cm. – (Routledge contemporary Southeast Asia series ; 69)
　Includes bibliographical references and index.
　1. Local government–Timor-Leste.　2. Nation-building–Timor-Leste.　3. Timor-Leste–Politics and government–2002–　I. Title.
　JQ790.A988.C84 2015
　320.8095987–dc23
　2014030753

ISBN 13: 978-1-138-49160-1 (pbk)
ISBN 13: 978-1-138-79635-5 (hbk)

Typeset in Times New Roman
by Out of House Publishing

This book is dedicated to my foster parents, Helen and Brendan Ginnivan, who taught me the value of community.

Contents

Acknowledgments   xii

1   The imperative to 'develop'   1
2   The making of political hybridity (a colonial history)   17
3   Democratisation   43
4   Local leadership   62
5   Dispute resolution   79
6   Economic relationships   96
7   Clientelism and patronage   114
8   Taking local politics seriously   131

Glossary   140
Index   141

Acknowledgments

This book would not have been possible without the support and participation of many others, including the many Timorese people who agreed to be interviewed, or who have in other ways participated in my research. To the various Timorese researchers who I have had the privilege of working with over the years – in particular, Abel Boavida dos Santos, Mateus Tilman, Alex Gusmão, Satornino Amaral, Vicente Maia and Maria Fatima Pereira Guterres – a warm *obrigada barak!* Special thanks go to my *'familia* Venilale', the Ximenes family, who welcomed me into their homes and their lives, and have taught me so much about their community and culture. Thanks also to the Canossian *madres* of Ainaro, who gave me a place to stay while I lived and worked in Ainaro in 2008–2009. My gratitude also to my PhD supervisor, Sarah Maddison, for her support while doing the original PhD research upon which this book is based.

Many thanks to those who read part or all of my book as it was being written, providing feedback, insights and encouragement: to Rui Feijó, Anne Brown, Clinton Fernandes and Laurentina 'mica' Barreto Soares, who provided academic feedback on sections of my book as they were developed.

And finally, a very special thanks to friend and editor, Rachel Hyland, who so generously gave her time and considerable expertise in reading my many draft versions, providing valuable feedback, support and assistance.

1 The imperative to 'develop'

Mainstream approaches to international state-building have typically not taken kindly to customary governance and law. Embedded in the state-building discourse is an assumption that 'development' necessarily involves the introduction of liberal democracy, human rights and economic growth, all of which can be nurtured through introducing new institutions that embody these principles. By this understanding, the creation of state institutions is considered a prerequisite for development, providing the right 'enabling environment' for democracy, human rights and economic growth to take hold (see for example North 1990). In pursuit of these overarching goals, customary governance is commonly considered irrelevant, or, alternatively, judged as an obstacle in reaching this vision of the idealised state.

But custom, and customary governance, is the lifeblood of many postcolonial communities. Around the world, billions of people cross daily between state-based and customary governance structures, ideals and norms. This postcolonial reality works in powerful ways to shape people's experience of themselves as citizens of the state, and as members of their culture and community – which in turn creates particular challenges for the government in appropriately meeting their needs. These challenges are not limited to nations in which international interventions have occurred, where the United Nations (UN) and other aid agencies have carried their development agendas. Rather, they are shared to varying degrees by most postcolonial states across the world, from nation-states with Indigenous minorities such as Australia or the United States, to nation-states where the colonising force has left the territory, such as Timor-Leste or Mozambique, to situations of postcolonial colonisation and differentiated autonomy such as parts of Indonesia or India. But despite the commonality of this experience, and the implications that it holds for both the government and its citizens, current approaches to state-building have been inept in dealing with this postcolonial reality.

The difficulty in recognising and engaging with the co-existence of state-based and customary institutions indicates that there is something fundamentally wrong with mainstream approaches to state-building and development. While state-building is premised on the creation of new institutions, policies and laws, a state is much more than its institutional framework. States are

2 *The imperative to 'develop'*

comprised of people, and people live in their own communities, according to their own cultures and worldviews, and modes of customary governance. This means that for state-building to be effective, state institutions must be responsive to community realities, and actively recognise and engage with pre-existing customary forms of governance. There are important reasons for this. When the institutions of the state are simply imposed from 'on high', rather than appropriately engaging and intersecting with community realities, the results are frequently traumatic for communities, and detrimental to the state more generally. One need only look at the experience of postcolonial minorities in developed countries, such as the Indigenous peoples of Australia, the United States, Canada and elsewhere, to see what can happen if cultural ways of being are pushed aside in favour of a new vision for the state. As these peoples exist in a context in which the overarching state and its economy is generally considered 'developed', but they themselves suffer conditions that are more comparable to that of a 'developing' country, their experience is instructive. In particular, it demonstrates that development for these communities involves much more than money, or the introduction of liberal democratic institutions. It also requires that the state recognise their culture and customary forms of governance, working with, rather than undermining, these sources of strength in a community. However, it seems that we have not yet learnt from these experiences. The history of international state-building and development is littered with examples where interventions carried out in the name of 'progress' have in fact weakened community resilience, undermining customary ways of life that have served people for centuries. It is past time to rethink these approaches to state-building, and consider new ways of engaging that respect the central place of customary governance and culture in postcolonial communities.

A central argument in this book is that institutional theory – upon which rests our understanding of constitutionalism, law and statehood – needs to be reimagined in order to properly account for the co-existence of state-based and customary governance. Mainstream approaches to state- and institution-building tend to conceive of state institutions as somehow separate from, and higher than, other social dynamics. It is a simplistic cause–effect approach, in which it is presumed that if institutions are created with sufficient force, they will naturally guide and shape human behaviour in logical and predictable ways. By this understanding, all other social forces, including customary governance, are seen and analysed through the lens of the state. Nevertheless, the reality in postcolonial communities is considerably more complex. There is a mutual shaping at play, in which communities need to be understood as not merely *subject to* institutions – but actively *engaging within* these institutions even as they are subject to them. This process of mutual engagement works in powerful ways to shape how institutions are applied in a community.

The ideas presented here are the result of five years' research on local governance in Timor-Leste, including an intensive period living in the mountain villages of Venilale and Ainaro in 2008–2009. During this time, I had the great privilege of becoming part of everyday community life, living and working in a context that was so different to my own. Every conversation and every experience helped me to understand different aspects of village politics and culture, while also framing these insights in such a way that they no longer seemed so foreign. The challenge for the research presented in this book has been to not sacrifice the many different viewpoints in order to produce a neat 'story'. At times, people's views were fairly similar, however at other times there were marked differences in people's ideas of legitimacy, good leadership, how things should be done within the community, and sometimes even on how things *were* done within their community. However, as my understanding of community dynamics progressed, underlying patterns and themes emerged to explain the differences in responses, as it became clear that people were balancing competing considerations in different ways. These insights led to the overall thesis of this book, that the requirements of co-existing state-based and customary governance are negotiated through everyday politics, as villagers endeavour to fulfil communal needs with available resources. For most villagers, the focus is not on whether an institutional solution to a particular problem is considered 'state-based' or 'customary'. Rather, the focus is on whether the institutional solution represents a legitimate and effective way of addressing the problem. Frequently, villagers will use a complex mixture of both to address community concerns.

Contemporary Timorese villages are characterised by a hybridity of state-based and customary values, laws and worldviews. Democratic ideals have taken hold in communities, and are embraced by villagers as part of what they fought for during the long struggle for independence. But *lisan*[1] is nonetheless central to community life. It is in this context that local leaders strategically engage with state-based and customary governance institutions in order to fill various community needs, and pursue their own individual political agendas. This simultaneous engagement of state-based and customary governance works to structure important aspects of community life, determining how community disputes are resolved, economic relationships formed and maintained, and leadership gained and maintained. This engagement happens as part of everyday local politics, giving us important insights into how social arrangements are shaped in the context of co-existing state-based and customary governance.

The ways in which power, politics, agency and oppression play out in local governing arrangements means that not everyone in the community has the same access to decision-makers, or to making decisions themselves. And for those who are most vulnerable, there is also a 'shadow side' to these everyday local politics. From a governance standpoint, the daily political decisions that are made by local elites effectively smooth the way for the state to operate in postcolonial communities by shaping the balance between customary and state-based governance. But these decisions also have a material impact on people's lives, as the interests of those who are most vulnerable are at times sacrificed to achieve this balance. Aspects of this dynamic have struck me many times in my research as existing inequalities relating to gender and class continue to be reproduced through the modern institutions of the state. As they enter the local political environment, these new state-based institutions are interpreted to fit with existing power relationships and customary governance norms – but they nevertheless retain their quality as 'modern' state institutions, clearly distinguishable from *lisan*. This serves to both deepen and legitimate those inequalities.

It must be remembered that customary governance is not static, and nor is the process of the hybridisation. As with every other social and political system across the world, customary Timorese systems of governance continue to adapt in response to internal and external pressures. When we examine the history of Timorese governance, we can see that what has evolved over time at the local level is a distinctly Timorese system, in which the rules and norms of *lisan* have alternately impacted on, and been impacted by, state-based systems of governance. As the new influences of liberal democracy and the capitalist economy are entering communities, this process of hybridisation is continuing, carrying with it challenges as well as opportunities for the Timorese government in attempting to create an inclusive democracy, and a system of government that is responsive to its citizens.

These experiences all hold important implications for how we understand state-building in a postcolonial context. Despite the intention of many would-be state-builders, the introduction of state institutions does not simply displace pre-existing customary governance norms and values. Rather, what results is a complex interplay of both, which can vary significantly from one community to the next. While the resulting hybridity comes about as a natural result of local politics, this does not mean that state decisions have no force. Quite the opposite: if state institutions work to undermine existing sources of strength in a community, the results can be quite destructive. On the other hand, if state institutions appropriately intersect with community realities and customary forms of governance, this can work to render state–society relations more coherent. The challenge is for Western-style liberal thinking to adjust its worldview and find the political space in which it can account for these other systems of governance that continue to hold primary legitimacy in local communities, working with and recognising the messy, complex process of hybridisation.

The international development industry

When we reflect on the various forms of hybrid governance that exist now, it is fair to say that both colonisation and the politics of decolonisation have changed the world dramatically. Throughout the second half of the twentieth century, as new countries emerged from colonisation with boundaries not of their making, embracing a mixture of ethnic and religious groups that often bore only a vague resemblance to traditional notions of communal and tribal identity, and grappling with a difficult and often violent history, the challenges of decolonisation have been met in various ways. In the early days of decolonisation in many countries across Africa, Asia and other parts of the world, hopes were high regarding what independence would bring to the previously colonised people. However, these high expectations were slowly replaced by disillusionment as it became clear that independence did not necessarily translate into a brighter future. International political and economic systems were often tipped sharply in favour of those already developed nations – the previous colonisers. In response, the newly independent countries formed the Non-Aligned Movement (NAM) as a vehicle to promote their unique political interests in the international arena, strategically using their majority presence in the United Nations General Assembly. Nonetheless, while NAM had many individual political successes, it did not successfully challenge the underlying power structures that disadvantaged its Third World member nations (Bandyuopahyaya 1977).

Just as importantly, in the newly independent nations it became clear that the spoils of independence and sovereignty over the nation's wealth were not going to be available to all citizens. Freedom and independence for most people did not mean access to more food, better health care, more jobs or better education. On the contrary, in many of these countries there were more conflicts and greater inequities and poverty. The impact of colonisation and the politics of decolonisation continue to resonate into the twenty-first century.

In the face of this reality, the question that continues to arise now concerns what is to be 'done' about the continuing poverty in postcolonial, developing nations. Are the features that block successful 'development' to be found in the political or economic systems of developing countries? Or in how aid is disbursed and trade is pursued? Is the key to be found in developed nations increasing aid? Or is it a case of developing nations needing to learn better tools of governance? These questions have become so consuming that an international aid and development industry, supported by millions of people and billions of dollars, has been created to explore possible new answers. It should be noted that while I refer here to the UN, international organisations such as the World Bank and International Monetary Fund, and various aid agencies, and to a lesser extent some non-governmental organisations (NGOs) who work in the state-building arena as all part of the 'development industry' in this context, these different organisations are by no means a homogenous group. In practice, they are often at odds with each other over both the process and the end-goal of development. What binds them together, however, is a commitment to state-building, however defined, and very often a similar set of assumptions over what development should look like. These assumptions need to be interrogated more closely.

It is a little strange that while we engage in lively debate over how the development industry should do its work, rarely do we question its underlying basis – the 'imperative to develop' – and to unpack what this phrase actually means. To question and analyse the premise of development itself appears to be the moral equivalent of saying that you believe that people should continue to live in perpetual poverty and insecurity. Yet the development industry, with its underlying premise that states must learn to develop, is a fairly recent phenomenon that only emerged in the middle of the last century. Before then, there were the disciplines of economics, of law and politics, of anthropology and cultural theory, of agriculture and health – and, of course, the theories underpinning different styles of colonisation. There was no discipline of development.

If we examine more closely the history of the development industry since decolonisation, fundamental to the various approaches is the hidden assumption that in order to 'develop', a state must move from customary or 'traditional' economic systems and political structures (which continue to thrive in many communities), and introduce the 'modern' system of capitalism and liberal democracy. This has given rise to a highly bureaucratic and project-based approach to development and democratisation that, as Ferguson (1990) notes, is strangely depoliticised and lacking in historical and cultural context. The assumption is that if aid agencies can come up with the 'right' mixture of 'good governance' practices for recipient states to follow, and NGOs can come up with the 'right' projects to implement, then development will naturally follow. The economy will grow. Poverty will be reduced. And human rights and democratic principles will be protected. Put another way, the assumption is that if we get the 'right' institutional mix – a complex task, but nonetheless still a mechanical problem – then society will be transformed in a predictable and positive manner.

This approach, however, flies in the face of all historical evidence on how economic progress and democratisation has proceeded in the West. The histories of liberal democratic countries are littered with revolutions and conflict, as the people fought to adapt their constitutional systems to reflect their changing cultural norms. Change was inherently messy, and through this process of conflict and negotiation, the changing political systems of the West, by definition, embraced the culture in which they were embedded. By contrast, the development industry has taken a very different approach, where the emphasis is less on political change through popular support and more on the bureaucratic approach of introducing a particular 'model' of liberal democracy through international intervention.

It is perhaps inevitable that this bureaucratic approach to development and democratisation would occur, given that international actors often have very limited mandates, and insufficient cultural understanding, to involve themselves in the internal politics of a nation. Nevertheless, when we examine recent history it is also clear that the results of transplanting depoliticised 'models' of democracy or statehood from the developed to the developing world have been patchy at best, leading many commentators to dismiss the value of international interventions (see for example Jenkins and Plowden 2006).

Questioning the value of international interventions, however, is not to say that all interventions have been a failure. To make such a claim would be a gross generalisation, as quite often, large sections of the recipient country actively seek international interventions, particularly when violent conflict is taking place and military support is needed to avert further bloodshed. Nonetheless, interventions in response to a crisis situation need to be separated from the longer-term objectives of 'development'. When we examine the nature of development and the assumptions underpinning it, we can see that many international interventions tend to come unstuck when the new institutions of government are negotiated and introduced to the population. The problems that arise are partly because these models are introduced by outsiders, with attendant issues of lack of understanding of the culture on the one hand, and resentment by the recipient population at being shut out of the process on the other. But the issues go much deeper than this. There are also very important and practical issues that arise when the institutions of Western-style liberal democracy are introduced in a political context where there are pre-existing customary laws, institutions and understandings of political community. When these models are introduced, the result is a complicated local governance environment in which state-based and customary governance, laws and institutions co-exist, interacting with each other in sometimes unpredictable and unstable ways.

This is by no means a new insight. Similar arguments have been made by numerous scholars, falling variously under the banners of comparative public administration (Riggs 1964), legal pluralism (Merry 1988), and development and legal anthropology (Oomen 2005; Shepherd 2009). Perhaps the most insightful work in this respect has been by scholars examining the governance of indigenous minorities in postcolonial nation-states (Tully 1995). For them, there has been no choice but to take the co-existence of customary and state-based governance seriously. However, these points have not been embraced by the dominant development discourse or utilised by development practitioners. Instead, what one tends to find is a conversation dominated by the normative question of whether customary governance is 'good' or 'bad', naturally progressing to the conclusion either that it should, or should not, be replaced with liberal democratic forms of governance – regardless of whether such approaches have been effective in the past.

'Good governance' theory: revisiting an old policy cycle

When we examine recent history, what we can see is a policy cycle that has played out since the early days of decolonisation, wherein trust is placed in the power of formal institutional transfer to promote some values over others – but to the dismay of an increasingly vocal movement against this approach, as the empirical evidence points out the underlying flaws.

As one tracks the history of cross-cultural institutional interventions, there is a sense of déjà vu to the ongoing debates over institutional reform, democratisation and good governance. Similar policy and academic cycles have been followed since colonised nations gained their independence after the Second

8 *The imperative to 'develop'*

World War. As these states emerged from colonisation, politically independent but with state boundaries and ideas of community and nationhood that had been externally imposed by their old colonial masters, new state structures were built that were intended to replace the colonial administration and bring together diverse communities to form a single nation. In most cases, the imposed concept of nationhood that presumed a certain cultural homogeneity did not reflect the internal diversity of these new nation-states.

Nevertheless, these quite distinct challenges were not given due recognition in the 'modernisation' agenda that prevailed immediately following decolonisation. As they became part of the 'international community', these new states were encouraged to nurture economic and political development following an 'evolutionary' modernisation agenda that worked from assumptions inherited from nineteenth-century European political theorists such as Max Weber and Ferdinand Toennies. As French economist Serge Latouche describes it, while the previous colonists gave up their direct administrative power they still retained a great deal of influence by their control over knowledge and development principles. Development, following the modernisation agenda, was to proceed on the pretension of a 'universalisation' of Western principles, transmitted by 'science, technology, economics and the mental outlook on which they all rested: the values of progress' (Latouche 1996, 17). Simultaneously with decolonisation, a development industry was born as modernisation theorists worked to find the best way to encourage economic and political development through finding the 'right' institutional mix.

However, it soon became clear that modernisation through the introduction of democratic political institutions did not go hand in hand with development and good government, and political scientist Samuel Huntington noted that in fact there had been an 'erosion of democracy' (1965, 392) that had taken place as modernisation had been pursued. As it became clear that the development industry was not living up to its promise, the underlying assumptions surrounding modernisation theory were rejected and a new school of thought known as 'dependency theory' emerged, which traced many of the problems back to modernisation itself (see for example Frank 1967).

A similar policy cycle was played out in the 1970s, as US aid agencies promoted a 'law and development' movement with an aim to creating a scientific approach to development. The emphasis was on improving legal institutions in developing countries, following a Western framework of liberal legalism (Merryman 1977). This movement was discredited when legal scholars David Trubek and Marc Galanter (1974), initially among the most vocal supporters of the law and development approach, argued that importing Western legal institutions to developing countries was ineffective because there was a fundamental conflict between liberal legalism and tribe and clan loyalties. This movement was short-lived; by 1977, John Merryman concluded that the 'law and development movement ... was bound to fail and has failed' (1977, 481). In his opinion, this failure could be put down to a number of factors, including 'unfamiliarity with the target culture and society (including its legal system), innocence of theory, artificially privileged access to power, and relative immunity to consequences' (Merryman 1977, 481).

Seen in this historical context, good governance purveyors are the most recent inheritors of this policy cycle that has played out since the end of the Second World War, when the development industry, in its contemporary form, began. The promotion of good governance through the introduction of political institutions attempts to bring together many different strands that are considered important in supporting a state's development, including the promotion of economic development as well as of political participation and representation through democratisation. Good governance theory was led in large part by institutional theorist and economist Douglass North's (1990) work into the relationship between political institutions and economic development, and the development of the New Institutional Economics (NIE). The main contribution of NIE was in pointing out the link between political institutions and economic development. This contribution was then taken as exciting new evidence of the importance of governance and institutional theory in guiding and nurturing development, and subsequently the school of 'good governance' was established. Across the development industry, various actors now commonly use this body of work to guide international interventions, promoting economic growth and encouraging stable governance environments.

To support this emphasis on good governance for developing nations, a great deal of effort has been put into developing universal indicators intended to measure governance performance. The World Bank was one of the first to promote this approach, with initial interest focused on the links between good governance and economic performance. This approach was soon adopted by other agencies, such as the Organisation for Economic Co-operation and Development (OECD) and the European Union (EU), and developed further by the United Nations Development Program (UNDP) to incorporate political aspects, linking good governance with democracy and the pursuit of human rights. The World Bank now has data from over 160 states since 1996, and assesses a combination of up to 300 indicators that are sorted according to six headline areas: voice and accountability; political stability and absence of violence; government effectiveness; regulatory quality; rule of law; and control of corruption. These indicators, or variations on these indicators, are the current 'tools of the trade' for the international community to assist post-colonial developing states to strengthen their institutional political, economic and social frameworks.

However, while the use of good governance indicators is accepted wisdom to guide institutional interventions, at least for the major actors who control most of the available funding, one of the main problems that has been identified across different measurement methods is the lack of clarity around the *definition* of good governance, and resultant variation and bias between and within sets of good governance indicators. The blurring between concepts that results from this definitional variation and concurrent lack of clarity has had very real consequences for Timor-Leste. During the UN interregnum from 1999 to 2002, the Common Country Assessment team for Timor-Leste established a broad framework based on theories of good governance intended to 'provide a template of principles on which to base the transition of East Timor to full independence' (UNDP 2000, 92). Their working definition for this template of principles was that 'good governance is participatory, transparent and accountable. It upholds the rule of law. It is responsive, equitable, and consensus-oriented, and efficient and effective in its mechanisms' (UNDP 2000, 92).

While these are laudable aims, and as overarching principles were no doubt developed to be much more specific in guiding the daily work of the UN, such a definition is nonetheless merely a listing of theoretical 'good principles' rather than a workable template for building governance institutions. In particular, as an overall philosophy guiding the UN's approach, it betrays a blindness to the complexity of institution-building in communities that operate according to very different cultural understandings, norms and values. As a result, it was not useful as a practical tool during the UN interregnum, tending to work more as a common language that shrouded underlying differences in approach rather than providing for a common policy agenda (Russell 2008). As different organisations such as the United Nations Transitional Administration for East Timor (UNTAET) and the World Bank used and interpreted 'good governance' to guide their work, the results varied widely and were sometimes contradictory – leading to a lack of coordination between these different actors and consequent negative effects for development of the newly independent nation (Russell 2008, 26–27).

In Timor-Leste, while there was already broad support for the principles of democracy, problems emerged as liberal democratic institutions were introduced without working through the paradigmatic differences between Western-style democracy and *lisan* (see for example Hohe 2002). This is not altogether surprising; the introduction of formal democratic institutions does not guarantee that they will be effective, nor does it assist in anticipating the consequences of these institutions as they are incorporated into the local political environment. While the bureaucratic approach to development has emphasised the use of specific models of 'good governance' to guide international interventions and development aid, the empirical evidence clearly indicates that what matters more is how those models are incorporated into the internal politics of the recipient nation.

This confusion in defining what constitutes good governance is further fuelled by the tendency to conflate democracy, human rights and good governance, forming a 'chain of equivalence' (Howarth 2000, 107), a device that works to rhetorically strengthen these disparate areas while simultaneously shrouding the relationships and tensions within and between these fields.

Similar points have been made by many other scholars and development practitioners, who argue against approaches to governance and institution-building that are apolitical and lacking in a nuanced understanding of the cultural and historical context. Cynthia Hewitt de Alcantara (1998), former Deputy Director and Research Coordinator at the United Nations Research Institute for Social Development (UNRISD), has warned against the tendency towards producing 'standard blueprint' models underpinned by technocratic understandings of good governance that shroud rather than illuminate the challenges faced within different political and cultural settings. Similarly, Kate Jenkins and William Plowden, each former political consultants for the UN, make a strong argument that good governance is in fact 'a flexible and highly ambiguous term which could be used to legitimise [Western] intervention in the internal management of recipient states' (2006, 64). This concern that good governance is simply a tool for the imposition of an external political agenda is also reflected in aid watchdog The Reality of Aid's critique that 'donors take an "Alice in Wonderland" approach to governance, so that it means whatever a donor wants it to mean' (Randel *et al.* 2004, 9), adding that 'many in the South ... are asking whether the donor concerns for "good" governance are no more than repackaged structural adjustment programmes' (Randel *et al.* 2004, 11).

Good governance indicators include many things that, to the Westernised perspective, seem to form good common sense. However, this common-sense approach is based on a particular worldview which emphasises – among other things – individualism and capitalism, which may not mesh with how communities see themselves, and may in fact be in opposition to their own, centrally-held values. Moreover, as discussed in the previous section, process is important. When applied from 'on high', following the depoliticised and culturally insensitive manner in which much of the development industry works, the good governance formula fails to engage with people's lived reality. At best, it can be seen as another form of cultural imperialism, which many postcolonial peoples are well-practised in adapting, subverting or ignoring. This means that it simply fails to 'stick', despite the billions of dollars spent on promoting this approach, enriching various international lawyers, policy specialists and consultants, but failing to improve the lives of everyday people in the villages. At worst, it can actually create new problems.

As this policy cycle has played out, academic debates have tended towards polarisation. On the one hand, the failure of institutional transfer has been explained as a result of the smuggling in of liberal democratic values through good governance theory, despite these values' incommensurability with the target culture and customary governance systems. On the other hand, there are claims that a state cannot 'develop' or 'advance' unless it leaves behind now-redundant customary systems of governance. Nevertheless, when we examine the lived reality in postcolonial communities, we can see that people are managing to engage with customary and state-based governance at the same time, in a fluid, ongoing basis. For them, it is not an either/or proposition. This cycling through old ideas, and failure to develop new knowledge, indicates that there is something fundamentally wrong with the debate itself. And it appears that this 'something wrong' comes back to the artificial binary of tradition and modernity itself. While the different positions on the policy cycle are poles apart, they share a common assumption centred on this binary, with the main difference being whether one sees customary values as something to be embraced – or discarded as an obstruction to development. However, the reality is much more complex. As we will see, different cultures, societies and communities are engaging with both at the same time, forming and re-forming their own unique identities in this most basic expression of self-determination.

Postcolonial realities

While development theory and practice may be premised on the idea that one must 'progress' from customary governance to liberal democratic forms of governance, this does not reflect the reality as experienced by billions of people across the world. As we have noted, for those living in a postcolonial state, crossing between cultures, and institutional structures is an everyday occurrence. And, like many other parts of the world, Timorese villagers have developed various hybrid models through which they endeavour to meet the various requirements of customary and state-based governance. As a result, and together with many other postcolonial nations across the world, what has emerged in Timor-Leste has not been a simple linear progression from customary to state-based governance. Instead, what continues to prevail is the messy co-existence of governance, institutions and laws that are sometimes mutually supportive and sometimes contradictory, but that are not easily matched one against each other, emerging as they do from very different worldviews. This messy co-existence is not new, and it cannot simply be explained away by insufficient time for democratisation to take hold and 'replace' customary systems. Indeed, if we examine Timorese governance history, it is clear that similar dynamics played out during Indonesian occupation and Portuguese colonisation as customary governance interacted with the governing institutions of the occupiers – and the occupiers, in turn, tried to either override or subvert the governance systems of the Timorese people (see for example Boavida dos Santos and da Silva 2012).

As we explore throughout this book, this simultaneous navigation of customary and state-based governance applies to various aspects of local governance, including how local authority is obtained and maintained, how that authority is exercised and shared, and how local leaders are ultimately made accountable for their decisions by the community. In the vast majority of cases, these hybrid models have not been introduced by policy or law-makers, or other actors from outside the community. Rather, they have formed as a result of local politics as the community has used the resources at hand to solve their problems. In some situations, these hybrid models have been developed by local authorities as a deliberate strategy to solve recurring problems in the community. In other situations, the model has come about more as a result of the many small, daily decisions that are taken by local leaders when doing their work. The common feature in all of these situations is that there is little attention paid to whether the resources used to solve a particular problem fall in the realm of 'customary' or 'state-based' governance. Rather, the guiding principles are whether the methods used will be embraced by the community (whether they will be legitimate), and whether they will be sufficient in solving the problem (whether they will be effective). Very often, these solutions will involve a complex melding of customary and state-based institutions, drawing on the worldview of both.

In Timor-Leste, there is a distinct lack of state penetration into most villages. State-provided services such as education and health are limited, and the police and courts are overwhelmed and under-funded. As a result, the primary source of governance in local communities tends to be *lisan*, and state-based institutions tend to be interpreted by villagers so that they do not undermine this system of governance. Sometimes, this means that existing understandings of the legitimate distribution of power and resources in a community are replicated into the new, state-based institutional form. This occurs, for example, in the very common scenario in which traditionally-legitimised leaders are elected to the *suku* council. Other times, when institutions have been introduced with the specific intention of challenging existing distributions of power and resources, these rules may be sidelined or ignored by large sections of the community. These dynamics can give a deceptive picture of the relative success or failure of formal institutional interventions. In situations where state-based institutions mirror existing relationships and distribution of resources according to *lisan*, they can appear quite strong but are in fact parasitic on customary governance arrangements. By contrast, where state-based institutions are built to challenge existing governance arrangements, they may in fact be slowly working and yet appear to be failing.

The practical results that are produced by these hybridised systems of governance are not always fair. Like politics everywhere, local politics in the villages of Timor-Leste is underpinned by an uneven access to power and resources. As local elites engage with each other and with those they govern, they draw on existing power bases and resources, interacting strategically with each other and making important decisions that shape their governance environment. Depending on the situation, some institutional requirements will be ignored or watered down just as others are emphasised, in a daily effort to maintain a balance between customary and state-based governance. Not everyone has the same level of influence in deciding which aspects are to be played down and which emphasised, and the interests of those who are most vulnerable may well be sacrificed in an effort to create and maintain this political hybridity as, day-by-day, it evolves and becomes entrenched. As such, there is a shadow side to these politics as existing inequalities are reproduced and legitimised in state-based institutions as they are incorporated into the local political environment.

When we compare this complex reality to the current approach embraced by the development industry, in which policy models are introduced with the expectation of predictable outcomes, we can see that these endeavours will always fall short. All social change is inherently political, and embedded in the particular cultural context of that society. This is the case at the national level, and is also the case within particular communities. And it means that when new institutions or policies are introduced, they are not being introduced into a governance *terra nullius*. There are structures and laws which exist already, and which are embraced by at least a good portion of the community because they fill certain needs. This means that we need to recognise and pay careful attention to the structures which already exist and the needs that they fulfil. But this is not the only implication. It also means that we need to recognise that the new structures will not simply replace the old in a natural progression from 'tradition' to 'modernity'. Rather, they will come together and interact with each other, and the ways that they interact will change over time and vary from one community to the next. This means that we need to change our focus from achieving predictable *outcomes*, to recognising and engaging with the *process* of interaction between different systems of governance. It is time for the development industry to catch up to this basic reality.

Development in a postcolonial context

The theoretical foundations which underpin contemporary development discourse do not tend to be helpful in understanding and analysing the process of hybridisation between state-based and customary governance. Instead, what we tend to find is that state-based and customary governance are often portrayed as binaries, and necessarily in opposition. According to this paradigm, customary governance is considered subject to the imperative to develop – and the primary mode of development has been to replace it with the liberal democratic institutions of state-based governance. This theoretical understanding fails to account for hybrid political systems in which customary and state-based governance co-exist in relatively stable patterns.

As discussed throughout this chapter, development theory provides no clear direction on how to understand and engage with political hybridity, because it has been unable to get past the unhelpful binary of tradition and modernity which lies at its core. This has meant that the questions that are being asked are often the wrong questions, and the policy solutions that are provided to answer these questions fail to hit the mark. Instead, as with many other parts of the world, the work of integrating these paradigmatic differences in Timor-Leste tends to be done within local communities themselves. While there is some official recognition that *lisan* holds important implications for state-based governance, in particular for criminal law and land tenure, existing policy frameworks are still unable to effectively engage with the questions of whether and how customary governance should be engaged when making policy. There is as yet no clear understanding in the international arena of how to 'build' state institutions in a manner that recognises, and is duly sensitive to, pre-existing governance systems.

It is interesting that despite heavy investment by the international community in learning how to 'do' development over the past half-century or more, there are few clear methods available to help the Timorese work through this particular set of challenges. But, as it is so closely related to issues of Timorese identity, perhaps this is just as well. Now, with the state being governed by an independent, democratically elected cohort of Timorese leaders, issues of what Timorese identity can and should look like are coming to the fore, bringing with them questions of how their identity as a nation should link with local identities. This has automatically prompted many questions relating to how co-existing structures should be dealt with, and what that means for decision-makers at the national level. These are all difficult, inherently political questions, which also have clear practical implications for people and how they live their lives.

Note

1 *Lisan* is often translated as traditional or customary law but is much broader than a legal system, encompassing many other aspects of morality and spirituality.

References

Bandyuopahyaya, J. 1977. 'The Non-Aligned Movement and International Relations', *India Quarterly: A Journal of International Affairs*, vol. 33, no. 2, pp. 137–164.

Boavida dos Santos, A. and da Silva, E. 2012. 'Introduction of a Modern Democratic System and its Impact on Societies in East Timorese Traditional Culture', *Local-Global Journal*, vol. 12, pp. 206–220.

de Alcantara, C.H. 1998. 'Uses and Abuses of the Concept of Governance', *International Social Science Journal*, vol. 50, pp. 105–114.

Ferguson, J. 1990. *The Anti-Politics Machine: 'Development', Depoliticisation and Bureaucratic Power in Lesotho*, University of Cambridge Press, Cambridge.

Frank, A.G. 1967. *Capitalism and Underdevelopment in Latin America*, Monthly Review Press, New York and London.

Hohe, T. 2002. 'The Clash of Paradigms: International Administration and Local Political Legitimacy in East Timor', *Contemporary Southeast Asia*, vol. 24, pp. 569–590.

Howarth, D. 2000. *Discourse*, Open University Press, Buckingham.

Huntington, S. 1965. 'Political Development and Political Decay', *World Politics: A Quarterly Journal of International Relations*, vol. 17, pp. 386–430.

Jenkins, K. and Plowden, W. 2006. *Governance and Nationbuilding: The Failure of International Intervention*, Edward Elgar Publishing, Cheltenham.

Latouche, S. 1996. *The Westernization of the World: The Significance, Scope and Limits of the Drive towards Global Uniformity*, Polity Press, Cambridge.

Merry, S.E. 1988. 'Legal Pluralism', *Law and Society Review*, vol. 22, pp. 869–896.

Merryman, J.H. 1977. 'Comparative Law and Social Change: On the Origins, Style, Decline and Revival of the Law and Development Movement', *The American Journal of Comparative Law*, vol. 25, pp. 457–491.

North, D. 1990. *Institutions, Institutional Change, and Economic Performance*, Cambridge University Press, New York.

Oomen, B. 2005. *Chiefs in South Africa! Law, Power and Culture in the Post-Apartheid Era*, James Currey, Oxford and University of KwaZulu-Natal Press, Scottsville.

Randel, J., German, T. and Ewing, D. 2004. *The Reality of Aid 2004: An Independent Review of Poverty Reduction and Development Assistance*, IBON Books and Zed Books, Manila.

Riggs, F. 1964. *Administration in Developing Countries: The Theory of Prismatic Society*, Houghton Mifflin, Boston.

Russell, T. 2008. *Institution Building Problems in East Timor, 1999–2002*. PhD Thesis published June 2008, Melbourne, Deakin University.

Shepherd, C.J. 2009. 'Participation, Authority, and Distributive Equity in East Timorese Development', *East Asian Science, Technology and Society: An International Journal*, vol. 3, pp. 315–342.

Trubek, D.M. and Galanter, M. 1974. 'Scholars in Self-Estrangement: Some Reflections on the Crisis in Law and Development Studies in the United States', *Wisconsin Law Review*, vol. 4, pp. 1018–1062.

Tully, J. 1995. *Strange Multiplicity: Constitutionalism in an Age of Diversity*, Cambridge University Press, Cambridge.

UNDP 2000. *Building Blocks for a Nation: The Common Country Assessment for East Timor*, UNDP and Team from other UN Agencies, Dili.

2 The making of political hybridity (a colonial history)

It has often struck me that the development industry's inability to deal with political hybridity reflects, at least in part, a lack of appreciation for history. History is what makes us who we are; it is detailed a complex. For international actors who will only be in the country for a short period of time, it is much easier to create something new than it is to build institutions based on historical context. For the Timorese, political hybridity is nothing new. Even a cursory examination of Timorese history demonstrates that Timorese communities are well-practised in navigating their own systems of customary governance, together with the governance system of overarching rulers. This chapter explores the complicated governance history of Timor-Leste, focusing on how political hybridity has been formed and maintained throughout almost 500 years of foreign occupation, through to present-day independence.

History can be told in many ways, and accounts of Timorese governance history have often described what the colonisers did *to* Timorese communities and systems of leadership. While these contributions are certainly important, they only tell part of the story. What is missing are accounts of how different communities have resisted, opportunistically responded, and creatively adapted to these external influences. Not all of these accounts are pretty. Alongside a history of often brutal colonisation and Timorese resistance, there is also a long history of Timorese oppression of other Timorese – sometimes with the help of colonisers, and sometimes without such help. This chapter does not purport to go into these different histories in any real depth; this should form the focus for a separate series of studies, preferably undertaken by Timorese scholars themselves. Here, it is simply worth noting that history has many sides.

Throughout the centuries, the centre of Timorese life has been small, kin-based groups, bound together through hierarchical systems of mutual exchange and governed via *lisan*. While the rules of *lisan* may vary from one group to the next, the centrality of *lisan* in defining how Timorese communities understand and govern themselves remains the same. These groups and systems of governance have operated in parallel with the governance structures of the external rulers, at various times being either reinforced or undermined by the imposed power structures – resulting in various forms of political hybridity that continue to be reflected in contemporary local governance arrangements. The interface that developed between *lisan* and the law of the colonisers was porous, as it is today, which means there were many different ways in which communities could adapt to external pressures while maintaining the core of who they were and are as a people. Where the interface was at its strongest therefore depended on political reality: balancing the colonial and Timorese rulers' needs against their practical ability (or inability) to control those communities that they claimed to govern.

Pre-colonial governance

Timor-Leste is sometimes referred to as a 'small half-island'. This is true: territorially, it is a small country. What is important about this description, though, is not so much the size of Timor-Leste as the fact that it encompasses only half of the island. The other half, Timor Barat or West Timor, is a part of Indonesia that until the 1960s was colonised by the Dutch.

Before Timor-Leste and Indonesia existed, with boundaries defined for the sake of colonial convenience, there was the island of Timor. The political structures that were in place, prior to Portuguese and Dutch arrival, consisted of small head-hunting kingdoms which were regularly at war with each other. According to various historical sources, there does not appear to have ever been a single overarching ruler of the island (see for example Capell 1944; Farram 2004; Fox 1982). In place of such a ruler there was the *Maromak Oan*, literally translated as Child of God, who presided over the ritual centre of Wehali, located in what is now West Timor. Many of the smaller kingdoms on the island were bound to this ritual centre and the *liurai* who ruled these kingdoms were answerable and paid tribute to the *Maromak Oan*. These *liurai* were all regarded as 'sons' of the *Maromak Oan* and were responsible for the political tasks of ruling the land and the people (Farram 2004, 37).

In contrast to the *liurai* 'sons' who presided over political matters, the *Maromak Oan*'s powers were spiritual in nature. He was deemed to have immense powers over the weather, defeat or victory in war, and the spread of disease. By this ancient view, real power came not from the material control over population and land, but rather from the spiritual powers of the *Maromak Oan* and the central significance of Wehali (Fox 1982). While relations between the different *liurai* 'sons' were often characterised by conflict and shifting alliances, this system of smaller kingdoms bound to a ritual centre provided overall stability (Farram 1999, 41).

It is difficult to form a complete picture of pre-colonial governance structures. However, there is strong evidence that the hierarchical political system headed by the *liurai* does not represent the 'original' political system of the island of Timor. By unravelling oral history, origin stories and linguistic clues, a number of historians claim that the *liurai* classes were actually a much later addition to Timorese social structures – which over time were incorporated into existing social structures through conquest and inter-marriage (Capell

1944, 197; Davidson 1994, 111–113). Together with oral history, this feature of Timorese history is most strongly indicated by variations on the Tetun terms *'liurai'* and *'datu'* which are used throughout the many different language groups of Timor, instead of each using different terms for different language groups, which one would expect had these classes evolved indigenously.

There are different theories on when and how the *liurai* and *datu* consolidated their rule in Timor. Together with the difficulties in unravelling unwritten history, it is likely that these regional variations reflect the unique circumstances of different clans. Shepard Forman (1977, 107–109), for example, claims that the *liurai* classes for the Makassae language group were descended from the Topass conquerors, a mixed group known as the 'black' Portuguese, and it was only through political and military alignments with the Portuguese government that they were able to establish their right to rule. By contrast, historian Kathryn Davidson (1994, 112) maintains that the *liurai* became a force in Timor much earlier, when the ancestors of the Tetun tribes forced the indigenous inhabitants to less fertile parts of the island and through conquest and inter-marriage established their rule. Given that the control that the *liurai* exerted over their tributary subjects varied significantly from one kingdom to the next, it is possible that both accounts are true for different parts of Timor.

If this account of Timorese history is true, this goes a long way towards explaining the very significant differences between an indigenous system of governance characterised by mutual exchange, and mediated by relationships within and between *uma lisan* (sacred houses), and the later arrival and hierarchical rule of *liurai* and associated classes, which is apparent in Timor-Leste culture even today. The *liurai* ruled via a class system that rigidly separated the Timorese into the classes of *liurai* (kings), *datu* (aristocracy), *ema reinu* (commoners), and *atan* (slaves), and were frequently at war with each other, competing for territory and tributary subjects. As Davidson also notes, it was an essentially 'outward looking' and expansionist system of governance (1994, 112). By contrast, the system of *uma lisan*, through which family groups related to each other via the customary institution of *barlake* or 'bride-price' – which establishes ongoing mutual obligations between families – was much more 'inward looking'. Access to land and riches was managed according to an individual's place within the *uma lisan* social structure, and one's place in that structure tended to only change with adoption or marriage. As a social structure, the *uma lisan* system was largely autonomous and self-governing, and as such, primary allegiance was owed not to the *liurai* but to the clan or kin group. By this account, the fundamental social units on which Timorese governance was built, and on which survival of the community depended, were these small, largely autonomous self-governing family units revolving around individual *uma lisan* (Davidson 1994). Reflecting on contemporary Timorese governance in light of this history, it is less surprising that even in communities where the *liurai*'s legitimacy has been lost, the system of *uma lisan* remains strong. While both the hierarchical rulership of the *liurai* and the system of *uma lisan* are important aspects of customary governance, they can also be separated – both historically and analytically.

While the *liurai* and *datu* were regarded as the 'natural' rulers and revered by the *ema reinu* who served them and paid them tribute, requests by *liurai* for tributes and warriors had to maintain a degree of fairness in order to be seen as legitimate. There were numerous cases cited by the Portuguese administration where the people had effectively removed themselves from a *liurai*'s rule and offered their loyalty to another ruler in situations where this fairness had not been maintained (Davidson 1994, 124). In addition, there were some *suku* communities that maintained themselves as independent and unaligned with any *liurai* (Sherlock 1983, 4). Even at that time, while not everyone lived within a kingdom under a *liurai*, everyone lived in a *suku* and knew their place within that clan, governed by the rules of *lisan* that were mediated through their *uma lisan*.

In a sense, it could be argued that the existence of the *liurai* classes provided a kind of 'buffer' to the impact of Portuguese conquest as they consolidated their presence. Despite the crushing brutality of the Portuguese against Timorese resistance, their colonisation left largely intact lower-order governance structures which tended to be inward looking. This meant that even towards the end of colonial rule in the 1970s, the Portuguese had very little to do with ordinary Timorese, except to extract taxes and labour, or if they were at war.

Early colonisation: sixteenth to nineteenth century

The Portuguese arrived in Timor between 1511 and 1515 after the conquest of Malacca (Capell 1944, 196). While it is often claimed that Timor was subject to colonisation for 480 years, such statements are misleading, as the Portuguese exerted very little control over the territory or the people until colonial consolidation in the early twentieth century. The early colonisers' focus was not on exercising colonial governance, but rather on harvesting sandalwood and converting the people to Roman Catholicism. Tellingly, it was the Dominican priests who were the first of the Portuguese to establish a permanent presence on the island in 1557, when they built a fort in Lifau, in what is now the enclave of Oecusse.

During those early days, the island of Timor was a site of colonial struggle between the Dutch, the Portuguese and the Topasses, or 'Black' Portuguese. While the Topasses retained some identity with the Portuguese from whom they were descended, they were an independent power group who varied allegiances to suit their own agendas (Boxer 1947). Each of these groups entered into strategic alliances with different *liurai* and waged 'proxy' wars with each other through these *liurai* as they fought for influence over various parts of the island. For their part, the *liurai* engaged in this struggle for a range of different reasons – in exchange for protection, greater power and/or riches, and to engage in their own wars, strategically using the Dutch,

Portuguese or Topass alliances to win new land and tributary subjects (Hägerdal 2009, 53–59).

Rather than terming it colonisation, which implies that the colonisers were able to exercise a certain level of control, the engagement at this time is best described as a case of ongoing power struggles between four elite groups: the Dutch, the Topasses, the Portuguese, and the indigenous elites, the *liurai*. Just as the *liurai* had regularly waged war on each other for land and tributary subjects, the newcomers also sought to expand their influence across the island through conflict and alliance. While the colonisers reported their various alliances as gaining 'vassals' for the kingdoms back in Europe, these relationships were seen very differently by the *liurai* who continued to form alliances and politically engage for their own purposes. Unsurprisingly for the people of the island of Timor, obligations and relationships through *lisan* held much greater significance than any claims of vassalage to a distant European kingdom. For example, historian Stephen Farram (1999, 43) describes how the Dutch vassals of Alor and Pantar (islands in what is now West Timor) habitually went to the ruler of Oecusse with whom they had a *lisan* relationship whenever there was a problem that needed external support. The fact that Oecusse was a vassal of the Portuguese and they were vassals of the Dutch held no significance for them.

As the wars went on, the Portuguese slowly gained more control. In 1642, the Portuguese and Topasses joined forces to march across the island to Wehali and burnt the settlement to the ground. The *Maromak Oan* was converted to Christianity and the great political and spiritual centre of Timor was defeated (Fox 1982, 22). In 1702, a formal seat of government was established in Lifau, located in the enclave of Oecusse. The first official governor entered into many alliances with the surrounding *liurai*, formalising these alliances by recognising their right to rule their own people, while simultaneously bringing them under colonial authority by bestowing military rank. This practice of militarily recognising Timorese rulers was very effective in cementing colonial influence, and continued well into the twentieth century (Boxer 1960, 353). The success of this practice was partly reflective of Timorese culture being an inherently warrior culture, and partly reflective of practical politics, as Timorese rulers who also had access to Portuguese forces were in a better position to pursue their own political interests. In 1769, the Portuguese were forced to retreat from Lifau to the new capital, Dili, as the Topasses and then the Dutch captured the territory (Capell 1944, 193).

Because the Portuguese did not have sufficient military might to conquer the *liurai* directly, they operated via a system known as 'indirect rule'. Indirect rule has been employed by various colonisers in many parts of the world, and worked by ruling through indigenous systems of governance – as opposed to direct rule in which the colonisers completely overruled indigenous systems and imposed their own system of governance. As was the case in Timor, the choice to manage colonial enterprises via indirect rule was often a matter of colonial convenience: when the coloniser could not muster sufficient force to overthrow the indigenous rulership completely, they would enter into an agreement whereby the king or chief would maintain control over his subjects in exchange for swearing fealty to the coloniser. Through these means, the Portuguese ensured a fairly loose colonial control over the territory, working through the *liurai* to extract riches and labour from the *ema reinu* when they required it.

This loose form of control exercised by the Portuguese began to shift during the nineteenth century, led in no small part by economic imperatives. During the early colonial period the Portuguese focus was almost entirely on the extraction of sandalwood, which did not require an intensive labour force. However, towards the turn of the nineteenth century, their focus moved to the harvesting of various crops for export, one of the most important of these exports being coffee. Compared to sandalwood, coffee is much more labour- and land-intensive, which in effect meant that the Portuguese needed to establish greater control over land, as well as better access to Timorese forced labour to work the large plantations (Davidson 1994, 19).

Unsurprisingly, as the Portuguese demanded more and more from the Timorese, they were met with great resistance by the *liurai* whose rule was being undermined, and by the *ema reinu* who were forced to fill these demands. Because of this resistance, by the end of the nineteenth century the *liurai* came to be regarded by the Portuguese as an obstacle rather than a support in achieving their desired aims. In response to this growing discontent, the governor took an incremental approach, tightening control through removing rebellious *liurai* from power and either incorporating them into allies' kingdoms or appointing a new, loyal *liurai* to replace one who had been rebellious (Davidson 1994, 98). These practices had a profound effect, which still reverberates in local communities: in a number of places where new people were appointed as *liurai*, often the traditional *liurai* continued to be recognised by the community as the 'real' *liurai*, effectively creating two *liurai* families where before there was only one.

In 1893, the governor followed this up by incorporating all remaining rebellious territories into military districts, provoking another series of uprisings (Davidson 1994, 183, 278; Dunn 1983, 19). Control was further tightened in 1906 when the Portuguese declared the customary tribute system unlawful, which was part of the system of mutual obligation between the *liurai* and their people (Davidson 1994, 103–104). This they replaced with the *capitação* (head tax), which was to be paid by the *ema reinu* directly to the Portuguese. The introduction of the head tax thus had two objectives: to support the growing colonial demands, but also to cut off the *liurais'* independent resource supply. This move caused great sadness in some areas, as the system of spiritual exchange between *liurai* and *ema reinu* was reinterpreted and its significance lost (Traube 1987, 121–122).

The Timorese response to these various measures was an ongoing series of rebellions across the territory, led by different *liurai*. These rebellions gained in momentum during the 1890s, and culminated in the major rebellion of 1911–1912, led by the *liurai* of Manufahi, Dom Boaventura. During this rebellion, Dom Boaventura successfully gained the support from many other *liurai* throughout Portuguese Timor and his rebellion is popularly characterised as *the* major anti-colonial rebellion; to claim lineage to these warriors is a mark of great pride. It was certainly the largest and longest revolt during Portuguese colonisation, resulting in around 90,000 Timorese deaths, extensive devastation of land, and finally concluding with the collapse of the independent authority of the *liurai*. While the customary authority of the *liurai* continues to exist to this day, the boundaries of the 47 kingdoms that existed in 1880 no longer played any role in the colonial administration (Capell 1944, 198). Following this defeat, the Portuguese divided the *liurais'* authority among the *datu*, or aristocracy, who had remained loyal to the Portuguese. These new authorities were then, confusingly, referred to as *liurai*.

To complement this new division of power, the smaller *suku* communities were administratively recognised for the first time, and their borders defined to better fit with Portuguese ideas of rulership and territorial control. This move represented a different form of violence to Timorese culture; as anthropologist Elizabeth Traube (1987, 100–101) relates in her study of Mambae culture, these new territorial definitions failed to appreciate traditional understandings of community, based around *uma lisan* that were often territorially distant from each other. In effect, these new administrative boundaries excluded many people from their traditionally-defined community because they now lived outside the *suku's* borders. This territorial definition, and redefinition, continued into the twentieth century. The effects of these administrative decisions continue to live on and resonate in contemporary local disputes around land and administrative divisions in many areas. For example, in a *suku* in Venilale, some of the elders appealed to the Prime Minister in 2007 to consider moving the *suku* boundaries back to where they were before the Portuguese split two *aldeia* from the rest of the community at the turn of the century. As one elder put it, their original *suku* had been split 'without justice or consideration by the white foreigner (Portuguese) ... and this now needs to be healed'.[1] However, this is opposed by other members of the community who do not wish to see their identities change again, or to deal with the land and administrative issues that would arise.

By 1916, the Portuguese had consolidated control over Portuguese Timor and extended their reach into the rural areas; people were now required to pay taxes and were pressed into service as forced labour. To complement this, they were also in the process of defining *suku* boundaries and *liurai* authority over these territories. Nonetheless, the Portuguese rarely extracted the taxes and labour from the people themselves; these tasks were given to the 'new' *liurai*. This did not make life any easier for the *ema reinu*, however, as the *liurai* were often more brutal in their treatment of their people than the Portuguese ever were (Dunn 2003, 19). With these various changes, the Portuguese policy of indirect rule became more of a mixed approach, in which power was still shared, but with much greater control over the *liurai* that they had chosen to rule on their behalf.

Over the years, indirect rule has been described in many different ways. In intellectual discussions during the later days of colonisation it was sometimes pointed to as an example of 'ethical' colonisation – a sentiment which is sometimes, concerningly, echoed in contemporary discussions. Here, the argument goes that because the colonisers did not interfere with the indigenous rulers' authority over their people, colonisation was less disruptive and therefore more ethical. This, nevertheless, fails to note the basic fact that to interfere with another system of governance, to support or to undermine authority, is to change it. Towards the end of Portuguese colonisation in 1975, there were many stories of *liurai* brutality against their people – and many people quite rightly mobilised against the *liurai* system. However, there is no knowing how powerful the *liurai* would have become without Portuguese, Dutch or Topass support. Equally, there is no knowing what customary checks and balances may have remained intact had the original system not been interfered with by colonial empowerment of the *liurai* through indirect rule. As such, there is no way of either assigning or avoiding colonial responsibility for some of the depredations of the *liurai* as they continued into the twentieth century. Examination of colonial history in Portuguese Timor demonstrates that claims of 'ethical' colonisation are naïve at best – and at worst, demonstrate a basic disregard for the history and culture of another people.

Portuguese colonial consolidation: 1912 to 1974

Portuguese Timor was always considered Portugal's poorest and most unimportant colony, and the consolidation of colonial rule did not translate into improved economic conditions for the Timorese people. While in some parts there was increased emphasis on coffee production, these were Portuguese enterprises designed to pay for the upkeep of the colonial presence in Timor. The years that followed the suppression of the 1912 rebellion and leading up to the outbreak of the Second World War saw Portuguese Timor described by former Australian consul James Dunn as 'undoubtedly the most economically backward colony in Southeast Asia, its living conditions often a subject of derision to the few who ventured to it' (Dunn 1983, 20). Increasing demands of head tax and forced labour took their toll, and meanwhile the Portuguese ran their colony with a bloated bureaucracy and little regard for the human or economic development of their colony – or even of upkeep of existing infrastructure. This lack of investment continued such that by the Second World War, Dili still did not have an electricity or water supply, no telephone (except for senior officials) and no paved roads (Dunn 1983, 20). It was not until 1970 that electricity was provided to Dili (Ramos-Horta 1987, 22).

From 1914 until the end of colonial rule in 1975, the Portuguese ruled via a dual legal system which separated 'unassimilated' indigenous people from 'assimilated' people. This required clearly separating people into various classes. 'Unassimilated' people comprised the majority of the population and were ruled by the *liurai* according to customary law, unless it was deemed 'contrary to natural law'. 'Assimilated' people comprised of five classes – European, *Mestiço* (mixed blood), Chinese, other non-indigenous (for example Goan or Angolan), and *Civilizado* (assimilated Timorese). These people were subject to Portuguese civil law rather than customary law, and enjoyed various other privileges associated with being considered Portuguese (Saldanha 1994, 76). While the Portuguese insisted that this system respected the place of customary law, again it came back to economics. What this framework of 'cultural respect' meant in practice was that the colonial administration could continue to demand forced labour from unassimilated Timorese, who comprised the majority of the population, with the claim that this reflected an aspect of customary obligations to the *liurai* (Davidson 1994, 49).

Portuguese colonisation was interrupted by the Second World War, when in 1942 the Allied forces entered Timorese territory, in defiance of Portugal's position of neutrality. While the Allied forces justified their presence in Timor as an anticipatory invasion, to prevent the Japanese from invading and controlling the territory, the result had the opposite effect of shifting Japanese attention to Portuguese Timor (Dunn 2003, 19). Various historical accounts demonstrate that had the Allied forces not first invaded Timor, it was unlikely that the Japanese would have been interested in the territory. The bravery of the Timorese who assisted the small number of Allied forces is well-documented, however they were poorly repaid once the Japanese gained control and Allied forces withdrew, with official estimates placing the number of Timorese deaths between the years of 1942 to 1945 at anywhere between 40,000 and 70,000 people. By the time the Second World War ended, the territory was devastated yet again.

In other colonial territories in the region, such as neighbouring Indonesia, the end of the Second World War essentially marked a new struggle for independence against their colonisers. However, this was not the case in Portuguese Timor. While there are some isolated instances of communities taking up arms after the Portuguese returned, there was no organised resistance, such as that shown by the Indonesians. This widespread resistance occurred much later in Portuguese Timor. Nonetheless, the Second World War marked the beginning of the end for colonisation worldwide and there were powerful decolonisation movements gaining momentum internationally. With this political reality, Portugal came under increasing pressure to deal with its colonies. Instead of giving up on their colonies entirely, the Portuguese began a set of reforms in 1960 which granted greater autonomy to their colonies, including Portuguese Timor. To complement these changes, the territory was divided into various administrative *concelhos* (districts), which in turn were divided into *postos* (subdistricts). Beneath the subdistrict continued the traditional communities of *suco* (village, or *suku*) and *povoação* (hamlet, or *aldeia*), although as noted earlier, the Portuguese definitions of *sucos* did not correlate with indigenous understandings of community. In 1964, a provincial Legislative Council was set up whereby the Timorese were actively involved for the first time in the administration of the colony. These Timorese Council members were initially appointed by the provincial governor, but slowly seats were included that allowed limited direct suffrage by the Timorese people. However, these reforms did not have a far-reaching impact, as the Timorese representatives tended to also be *liurai* – the same people who relied on Portuguese rule to prop up their own power, and who therefore had little to gain by pushing for independence (Dunn 1983, 35–36). It was not until 1974 and the overthrow of the fascist regime in Portugal that any serious, organised opposition in Portuguese Timor emerged (Dunn 1983, 5).

In the final days of Portuguese colonisation, the provincial and local levels were administered through 13 *concelhos*, under which operated 60 *postos*. Each *concelho* was administered by the *administrador do concelho*, beneath whom operated the *administrador do posto*, who was sometimes also known as the *chefe de posto*. Beneath these figures were the *chefe de suco* and then the *chefe de povoação* (Saldanha 1994, 52). Administratively, the Portuguese strictly limited the powers of the *chefe de suco* and *chefe de povoação* to receiving orders from the *chefe de posto*, collecting taxes and resolving local disputes, which, with the exception of murder, were resolved through the traditional council of elders (Hicks 1972, 101–102). Using the customary authority figures of *chefe de suco*, *chefe de povoação* and the traditional council of elders was no doubt a deliberate strategy. As Timorese economist João Saldanha (1994, 52–53) notes, as a very poor nation Portugal was having troubles of its own, and administering a system through existing structures and with existing resources was the cheapest possible solution.

Customary governance systems remained strong so that even by the late twentieth century at the provincial and local levels there remained what anthropologist David Hicks (1983), who lived in Portuguese Timor prior to Indonesian invasion, described as an 'unachieved syncretism' between customary and Portuguese governance. The central figure in the colonial system was the *administrador de posto* (subdistrict administrator), who was an official of the Portuguese government. While the *liurai* continued to be recognised and given significant power, by this time they needed approval from the *administrador de posto* before being appointed as king, and when making important administrative decisions (Forman 1980, 340).

Emergence of a new politics, political parties and civil war: 1974 to 1975

While the Portuguese were grossly neglectful of their least important and farthest-flung colony, there were some significant changes that occurred towards the end of their rule in Portuguese Timor. Perhaps the most noteworthy change was in the spread of educational opportunities for Timorese children: in 1953 there had only been 8,000 children in 39 primary schools, but by 1974 this had risen to almost 60,000 students in 465 schools. Better educated Timorese meant access to more powerful positions in the colonial administration, and by 1974 approximately 60 per cent of all *administradors de posto* were Timorese (Dunn 2003, 7). These officials knew too well the despotic power that was exercised by many *liurai* and often actively worked to reduce their power, in favour of progressing towards a more democratic system of government. These newly emerging political elite were among the first to become politically active in 1974, when it became clear that Portuguese colonialism was drawing to a close.

The 1974 Carnation Revolution,[2] which led to a new democratic system in Portugal, also marked the official beginning of decolonisation in Portuguese Timor. As Portugal prepared to withdraw from its remaining colonies, a strong independence movement led by a new Timorese elite began to develop. Although the formation of political parties was still illegal in theory, two major political parties – *União Democrática Timorense* (UDT) and the *Frente Revolucionária de Timor-Leste Independente* (Fretilin) – and one smaller one – *Associação Popular Democrática Timorense* (Apodeti) – were founded in 1974. Despite their formal illegality, these new parties were nonetheless given de facto recognition by the Portuguese administration in Dili, which allowed this as an important step towards facilitating decolonisation (Nicol 2002, 56).

Once the decision was made that the Portuguese would withdraw from Portuguese Timor, things moved very quickly. This left little time for the different political parties to prepare. Unsurprisingly, the major point of difference between the three parties regarded how decolonisation should proceed. Apodeti favoured integration with Indonesia as an autonomous state, and UDT and Fretilin favoured full independence but with different timelines for Portuguese departure. The different political parties also reached out to different constituencies. Apodeti, as the most conservative political party, were able to attract the support of a number of *liurai*. UDT, as the more conservative of the two major parties, also worked on gaining the support of the *liurai*, as well as the administrators and subdistrict administrators. Fretilin chose to focus mainly on the ordinary people, or *ema reinu*, at the community level (CAVR 2006a, 24–25).

If the emerging Timorese leaders were politically inexperienced, the exposure of the ordinary Timorese to party politics was that much worse. Many people did not understand these new politics and stated that they had joined their political party 'because others in their family had done so' (Nicol 2002, 156). The hasty progression to decolonisation had left no time for education of the Timorese on what independence and self-government would mean, and what the new political parties stood for. There was little time to introduce the idea of peaceful political competition. Instead of a gradual process in which non-violent party-political competition was introduced to the people, what came about was a war of words that soon disintegrated into violent conflict. The confusion and fighting was exacerbated by the Indonesians, who were using radio broadcasts and other means to spread disinformation and inspire fear among the people, in preparation for the invasion they were to carry out a few months later.

As these politics reached boiling point, pushing the parties further and further apart, the violent rupture of civil war was prompted by a coup that was mounted by UDT, and opposed by Fretilin. As analysts at the time noted, the difference between the policy platforms of the two parties was relatively minor, with Nicol (2002, 156–173) describing the most obvious difference between the parties at this stage lying in a 'politics of hate' that had developed, rather than any clear distinction in what they stood for. However, by the time civil war did break out, the hate was very clear and there were atrocities committed by both sides. As noted by the Commission for Reception, Truth and Reconciliation in Timor-Leste (CAVR), 'the brutality of East Timorese people against each other in this brief conflict has left deep wounds in East Timorese society which continue to be felt to this day' (2006a, 43). Across many communities in Timor-Leste, people still speak of different events during the civil war that are as yet unresolved, creating deep divisions and turning families against each other. These unresolved issues continue to form part of the underlying local patterns of violence, which are reinvigorated when new issues arise and conflict re-emerges.

Decolonisation has rarely been done well. In most cases across the world the colonising force has left too abruptly (and often only when they were pushed out), leaving their erstwhile colonial subjects to pick up the pieces as best they could. Such was also the situation in Portuguese Timor, where there is certainly a case to be made that the Portuguese could have done more to prepare the Timorese for independence. By the time the civil war broke out, however, the Portuguese administration could do very little to stop it. Dunn paints the picture vividly: as the two forces converged on Dili 'the tiny Portuguese force of fewer than 100 combat troops was wedged between 1500 UDT soldiers and more than 2000 regular troops under Fretilin command' (2003, 150). When Fretilin overcame UDT forces and made a unilateral declaration of independence, there was widespread panic, fanned by Indonesian radio broadcasts from West Timor giving 'exaggerated and distorted descriptions of the fighting', peppered with 'false accounts of atrocities and brutalities, most of which were attributed to Fretilin' (Dunn 2003, 153). Under the pretext of 'stabilising' their close neighbour and ensuring the violence did not spill over into Indonesian territory, Indonesian troops invaded East Timorese territory on 7 December 1975.

It is clear that the possibility of a smooth transition to independence was undermined by a hasty decolonisation, and the political manoeuvring of Portugal and Indonesia. It was also undermined by the disenfranchisement of the emerging Timorese leadership as active participants in decolonisation. This was clearly seen in a conference that was convened in Rome, aimed at ending the civil conflict which included the Portuguese and Indonesian foreign ministers, but ironically excluded the East Timorese (Ramos-Horta 1987, 59). The end result was that the Timorese had a tragically short few months in which to attempt to negotiate the multiple demands of decolonisation and independence, establish their political parties and policies, and balance multiple interests in either preserving or changing the status quo, all in the context of the Portuguese desire to decolonise as quickly as possible and Indonesia's disinformation campaign. As well as the deep psychological scars that this and subsequent violence has left on Timorese communities, the politics of hate and its association with political parties continues to be an important aspect of contemporary governance at all levels from the national to the local.

Timor Timur, the '27th province' of Indonesia: 1975 to 1999

The Indonesian forces invaded Dili on 7 December 1975, followed up by an attack on Baucau three days later. The randomness and savagery of these attacks have been well-documented and these events set the tone for future murders, torture, rapes and other atrocities that were carried out during the 24 years of Indonesian occupation (CAVR 2006b). As the first step towards legitimising their annexation of Timor-Leste, the Indonesian authorities announced that on 31 January 1976 all political parties had 'dissolved themselves', to be replaced by three officially sanctioned Indonesian parties (Saldanha 2008, 70). Following a farcical 'vote for integration' and in a process that shut out even Apodeti, the party which had desired integration with Indonesia, on 17 July 1976 Timor-Leste officially became the '27th Province' of Indonesia. This annexation was never recognised through international law.

Following this successful invasion by the Indonesian military, Timorese governance structures were brought into line with that of other parts of Indonesia, and trusted pro-Indonesia Timorese were appointed to positions of authority within the new structure. At the provincial and local levels, the Indonesians largely adopted the existing district and subdistrict boundaries, integrating them into Indonesian local government administrative divisions. In addition to this, the Indonesians formally recognised the previously unrecognised governing units operating at the levels of *suco* and *povoação* (Saldanha 1994, 102–103). Popular elections were introduced for the *suco* chiefs in 1982, however, given the ongoing presence and brutality of the Indonesian military, the democratic credentials of these elections were highly questionable. The *povoação* chiefs continued to be appointed following customary processes and their power was fairly limited. In theory, incorporating these levels into the state structure as part of the Indonesian administration should have given them more opportunity to implement village programmes. Nonetheless, as Dunn relates, the appearance of Timorese rule was a thin façade. As Timor-Leste was under heavy military occupation, the most powerful person at every level of governance was the military commander (Dunn 1983, 301).

Those who had been able to escape the Indonesian invading forces had fled to the mountains under Fretilin's leadership. As well as defending these groups, Fretilin arranged for crops to be sown and medicinal herbs to be grown, and prepared makeshift medical centres. Following mounting Indonesian military pressure and a rift in Fretilin leadership, and faced with the option of surrendering or starving, many people were forced to surrender themselves to the Indonesian authorities and went to live in the concentration camps, euphemistically named 'resettlement centres', that had been established in the lowlands (Taylor 1999, 85–88). Conditions in these camps were very difficult, food was scarce, and sanitation and health care were of a poor standard. This, coupled with tight restrictions on freedom of movement for those within the camps which impacted their ability to tend crops, brought on a famine of devastating proportions. Thousands of Timorese died of starvation and disease during this time.

The 24 years of Indonesian occupation were extremely difficult. While the restrictions imposed in the early years were eased slightly in some areas as the occupation progressed, in other areas – labelled 'red zones' – they remained much the same throughout. Regardless of whether or not they were in a red zone, most Timorese were effectively shut out of any potential engagement in the economy or the political system (Saldanha 1994). In addition, the people had very little capital to build on, as their homes and property before the invasion were often destroyed, and their land arbitrarily reallocated to those who were loyal to the Indonesians. This made life very difficult.

In contrast to Portuguese neglect, infrastructural development increased during Indonesian occupation, with more roads, community health centres and senior high schools built in almost all subdistrict towns (Mubyarto *et al.* 1991, 3). However, such 'development' in the midst of a military occupation was a thin veneer, and often used as a way to counteract local reactions to military excesses. As one villager in Venilale described it to me, 'where there was a killing, tomorrow there would be a new well'.[3] Besides the brutality displayed by the military, the administration was highly corrupt. There were numerous complaints made by aid workers, when they were finally allowed into the territory by the Indonesian authorities in the early 1980s, that food and medical supplies intended for the Timorese were being diverted to private business (Dunn 1983, 338; Taylor 1999, 120–122). These concerns over corruption did not just apply to foreign aid; even as Indonesia turned its focus to providing more development into the territory, many projects were abandoned before completion, together involving multi-billion US dollar outlay. In 1994 alone, there were 465 cases of corruption reported (Saldanha 1994, 344–345). Given the fear that the Indonesian military inspired in the general population, there is little doubt that many other such cases went unreported.

The disenfranchisement of the Timorese under Indonesian rule was further heightened by the influx of migrants from other parts of Indonesia, facilitated through an Indonesian transmigration programme – a deliberate strategy of social engineering designed to dilute the Timorese resistance to Indonesian rule (Gunn and Huang 2006, 68). Many of the newcomers took on positions of authority within the Indonesian administrative and military structure and others took over monopolistic business interests in Timor: for example, one of the largest consortiums, set up by several generals immediately following the Indonesian invasion, held a monopoly on logistical support for the military (Saldanha, 1994, 346). Similarly to the Portuguese colonial period, the Indonesian combination of military might with monopolistic business meant that the East Timorese were effectively shut out from the economy. Even 15 years after integration, the constant presence of the military, and their interference with development initiatives through protecting and encouraging monopolisation, was regarded by most Timorese elites as an insurmountable impediment (Mubyarto *et al.* 1991, 61).

These combined factors had the effect of hardening local attitudes against Indonesian occupation. The Timorese had no access to decision-making within the Indonesian administration, and when they did, they found that they could achieve very little because of the oppressive military presence. Participating in the independence movement, by contrast, was an active way through which they could assert their identity and assist and encourage the resistance fighters in the mountains. The brutality of the military, combined with the disenfranchisement of the Timorese from real economic or political engagement, gave a strong incentive for ordinary Timorese to actively contribute to the resistance movement.

Throughout this time the armed resistance, named FALINTIL (*Forças Armadas da Libertação Nacional de Timor-Leste*), continued to mount offensives against the Indonesian military, and were supplied with food, medicines and information by the villagers in the resettlement zones through their clandestine networks. While initially the resistance movement was dominated by Fretilin's leadership, this changed in the 1980s, when key leaders reorganised the resistance to incorporate other political parties and perspectives (Gusmão *et al.* 2000, 131–132). In an effort to be more inclusive, they declared the military arm to be independent from any political party, and representative of all Timorese in the broader independence struggle. This political reorganisation was accompanied by a transformation of the resistance itself into a network of smaller, more mobile units, incorporating both guerrilla fighters and village clandestine operatives, and with a strong international following (Gusmão *et al.* 2000). Many Timorese within the villages became actively involved in the clandestine movement that protected and provided resources for the FALINTIL fighters in the mountains.

As anthropologist Andrew McWilliam (2005, 35) relates, key to the clandestine movement were the *suku*-based leaders of networks known as the *núcleos de resistência popular* (*nurep*). *Nurep* were popularly elected by representatives from all *aldeia*, with the election conducted by a FALINTIL commander. *Nurep* were effectively the clandestine counterpart to the Indonesian-recognised chief of the *suku*, the *kepala desa*. Beneath the *nurep* were the *aldeia*-level clandestine networks, the *selcom* (or *selular comunicação*). There was also a clandestine subdistrict chief, *secretario de zona*, who was chosen by FALINTIL commanders (Ospina and Hohe 2001, 58–59). As McWilliam (2005) relates, this clandestine structure of *selcom*, *nurep* and *secretario de zona* had two distinct advantages. First, these small networks meant that if one member was compromised it would not endanger the wider clandestine operation. But second, perhaps more importantly, it deliberately capitalised on existing understandings of community, in which Timorese extended family networks are bound by *uma lisan*, and which form the basis for *aldeia* and *suku* communities. The reliance of the clandestine operation on family networks was clearly recognised by the Indonesian military and reflected in the 1982 'Instruction Manual' that was produced to guide Indonesian intelligence operatives – a total of nine documents, in which detailed instructions were given on how to break the clandestine movement through interrogating family members of resistance fighters, and subverting the continuing influence of the *liurai* (Budiardjo and Liong 1984, 179–194).

In addition to the clandestine network of *selcom*, *nurep* and *secretario de zona*, there was a growing student resistance movement as a new generation who had grown up under occupation began to organise, linking in with the pro-democracy student activists in Indonesia. This student resistance movement climaxed with a series of events and protests that led to the Santa Cruz massacre, as mourners attending the burial of an activist were gunned down in the cemetery on 12 November 1991. This brutal event was filmed by British journalist Max Stahl and spread throughout international media outlets, sparking popular outrage across the world. Following this tragedy, Timorese leaders such as Catholic Bishop Belo began to argue their case for the autonomy of East Timor, similar to that which had already been granted to Aceh and Yogyakarta. In 1996, Bishop Belo and Timorese diplomat and former President José Ramos-Horta were co-recipients of the Nobel Peace Prize – an indication of the increasing international attention that was being brought to bear on the 'East Timor question'.

Meanwhile, the Indonesian pro-democracy movement was gaining ground and, in May 1998, Indonesian President Suharto was removed from office. This provided the political window that the pro-independence movement had been looking for, and in April 1999 an agreement was signed mandating the United Nations (UN) to conduct an election on the future status of East Timor – independence, or special autonomy within Indonesia. The elections were conducted in an atmosphere of extreme violence and intimidation, led by pro-Indonesian militia who were secretly armed by Indonesian forces. However, despite the murders, house-burnings and other tactics that were taken to undermine the elections, on 30 August 1999 the Timorese people overwhelmingly voted for independence. They did this, knowing that independence would be achieved at great cost. Following the vote, the military and militia deported 250,000 people across the border, killing or 'disappearing' at least 1,400 civilians (CAVR 2006b, 19). Despite documents that were intercepted prior to the vote, showing that pro-independence voters would be 'punished' after the election, UN and Allied forces withdrew, leaving the Timorese to face the consequences alone (Fernandes 2004, 74–81). Considering the size of Timor-Leste, with a population of only a little over a million people, this effectively meant that there was no one in the territory left untouched. The post-election violence continued unchecked for two weeks, until it was stopped by the arrival of armed international forces on 15 September 1999.

The impact of Indonesian occupation on local political structures was complicated. The brutality of it and the struggle for independence from it had the effect of sharply delineating the Timorese family networks and customary governance structures from the authority structures of the Indonesian state, making engaging in and celebrating their culture an important aspect of Timorese resistance. In addition, as FALINTIL actively utilised the networks of trust that existed through relations within and between *uma lisan*, these too became an integral part of the resistance. Nonetheless, Indonesian brutality and their use of Timorese militias has also left deep psychological scars, turning family against family, and introducing new animosities.

In addition, the Indonesian occupation deepened already existing tensions between families and communities at the local level. Timorese affiliation with militias was not random and there were cases of militia violence that could be traced back to feuds that had existed for over a century, with violence on both sides (see for example Gunter 2007; Rawski 2002, 84–93). In this context, Indonesian brutality provided a new outlet for settling old scores, a feature that the Indonesians deliberately played on in recruiting militia members. The fact that the military objectives of the Indonesian occupying force were translated into local politics also provided a convenient excuse for the Indonesian military, who subsequently denied responsibility for the actions of the Timorese militia who acted on their behalf. This legacy of violence, and the continuity of violent conflict between communities, cannot be underestimated, as it has left deep divisions within many Timorese communities.

The legacy of this period still strongly resonates in local communities. On the one hand, local and national leaders often source their political legitimacy through referring back to the part they played in the resistance. The respect that is given to veterans as political leaders is just as (if not more) important as the respect which is given to cultural leaders. Very often, these different sources of legitimacy combine so that a single leader can claim both cultural legitimacy and legitimacy as a veteran. In addition, the hierarchical structure of the resistance and the hierarchical structure of customary governance serve to reinforce each other. Local leaders who can claim cultural legitimacy and/or who were leaders in the resistance are in a strong position, and if they so choose can be quite dictatorial in their approach with the knowledge that other members of the community will follow.

Rebuilding: UN interregnum

With the vote for independence came a whole new chapter for the Timorese, and many competing demands which needed to be met. Security needed to be re-established, a functioning civil administration needed to be put in place, essential infrastructure needed to be rebuilt and the immediate needs of the traumatised population attended to – and everything needed to be done immediately. To meet these various requirements, on 25 October 1999 the

United Nations Security Council passed UN Resolution 1272, establishing the United Nations Transitional Administration in East Timor (UNTAET). In recognition of the tricky task ahead, UNTAET was granted an unprecedented amount of power, almost equivalent to that of a sovereign state.

There is no doubt that UNTAET had their work cut out for them. One of the issues that arose early and was never adequately addressed was how to incorporate Timorese voices into the crucial state-building decisions that were being made. In a first attempt at 'Timorisation', in late 1999 UNTAET established the National Consultative Council (NCC) to facilitate Timorese participation in the rebuilding. However, their decision-making powers were limited and most Timorese leaders believed that it was no more than a rubber-stamp body (King's College 2003, 98; Rodrigues 2003). Many of the leaders refused to participate, and continued to be vocal about their lack of real inclusion. To remedy this growing discontent, in late 2000 the NCC was replaced with the National Council (NC), which had expanded decision-making powers.

Nevertheless, the creation of a council with expanded powers did not fix the problem. Of course, there was a question over the level of decision-making power that UNTAET should share with the Timorese – but there was also a question of *who* among the Timorese should be making those decisions. While the struggle for Timorese independence had been premised on the perception of a united liberation movement, this did not reflect the reality of Timorese leadership during the occupation (da Costa Guterres 2006). By the time independence came, there were many different factions in the Timorese leadership, who were sometimes bitterly opposed. UNTAET, however, was largely unaware of this reality. As Juan Federer, who had worked for a long time with Jose Ramos-Horta in the independence struggle, noted, UNTAET's strategy was insufficiently sophisticated to deal with the multi-factioned leadership, and they struggled to include anyone who did not speak English or Portuguese. As they came under increasing pressure to include Timorese decision-makers, UNTAET began to turn more to the National Council of Timorese Resistance, or CNRT, as a constituency that could help them with Timorisation. However, CNRT was dominated by the Portuguese-speaking older generation of leaders who had fled the Indonesian invasion. This effectively excluded many of the younger Indonesian-speaking leaders who had grown up under occupation, who did not speak the languages of UNTAET (Beauvais 2000, 1123; Federer 2005, 88).

Just as importantly, there appeared to be little understanding of the disconnection between the elites who were engaging in national politics and the majority of the population, mainly living subsistence lives in the rural areas. The CNRT was dominated by returned Timorese diaspora from Mozambique, Portugal, Australia and other countries, who had little in common with the Timorese who had remained on their lands. While they could clearly see many problems that needed to be addressed, there was little recognition of the very different worldview of people in the villages, whose only experience was of customary governance and Indonesian oppression. This disconnection between the Timorese elites in Dili and the majority of the population in the rural areas was also fuelled by the UN's focus on economic development that failed to reach beyond Dili, coupled with a failure to establish effective communications and transportation systems which might conceivably have stemmed the growing rural/urban divide. Federer's concerns were echoed by Jarat Chopra (2003) who served as the Head of the Office of District Administration for UNTAET, and argued that the majority of Timorese were being excluded from UNTAET's state-building efforts, effectively laying the foundations for future conflict.

UNTAET's approach was highly centralist. While the administrative structure included District Administrators (DAs) that were assigned to each of the 13 districts, and District Field Officers (DFOs) who were assigned to the 65 subdistricts, the reality was somewhat different. The rejection of a request for administrators to be appointed to support the overworked DAs meant that the DFOs, who were in theory responsible for operating at the subdistrict level, were in most cases redirected to work at the district level (Chopra 2003, 988). Not only was UNTAET's deliberately weak regional structure the source of serious criticism because of its impact on local participation, Terry Russell (2008, 157) also notes that UNTAET continued on this course even though they were openly aware it was not an appropriate model for the Timorese. In effect, the tricky issues surrounding administrative devolution of power and local participation in governance were left unattended, to be picked up by the Timorese government come independence.

Given UNTAET's lack of interest in local governance, the hiatus in local-level leadership was filled by the CNRT *nurep* networks. In most places, as the people began to emerge from hiding in late 1999, a *nurep* was put in place as *chefe de suco* to keep order in the *suku*. This was arranged by agreement between FALINTIL and CNRT representatives and the village elders. In September 2000, this was followed up by a popular election for the *chefe d'aldeia*, which was conducted by the *chefe de suco*. At the same time, the World Bank began its Community Empowerment Program (CEP), designed to simultaneously encourage democratic decision-making and distribute much-needed resources at the local level. Under the CEP, 416 *suku*-level Village Development Councils were established, to which over 6,400 councillors were directly elected by villagers in over 3,000 separate elections that were held in *aldeia* across Timor-Leste (Ospina and Hohe 2001, 83). Each Village Development Council was established on a 'one man-one woman' basis.

However, the CEP hit a number of administrative road-blocks. UNTAET was hostile to the idea of Village Development Councils from the beginning, fighting hard to block implementation of the programme in 2000 (Chopra 2003, 992–994; Russell 2008, 157). This had flow-on effects with a lack of communication and coordination between CEP facilitators and UNTAET DAs, so that in some cases DFOs did not even realise that CEP came under UNTAET's auspices and hence had no sense of loyalty to the programme (Ospina and Hohe 2001, 129–130). More importantly, the Village Development Councils suffered from lack of local legitimacy within the villages. To dovetail into the CNRT elections for village chiefs, the CEP excluded these chiefs from election to the Village Development Councils. Traditional leaders were also ineligible to sit on the councils. This proved to be a highly controversial decision, and while Jarat Chopra and World Bank anthropologist Tanja Hohe suggest that the rationale was to maintain a separation of powers at the local level (Chopra and Hohe 2004, 296–297), development worker Ben Moxham took a more cynical view, arguing it represented 'a "civilising" mission: a way to bring a "one-size-fits-all" democracy to the countryside' (2005, 524).

Regardless of the intent of this policy, it ultimately proved to be a key weakness. In addition to the exclusion of legitimate leaders, the World Bank's requirement that CEP members be literate meant that mainly young literate people were elected onto the councils. However, these young people tended to not come from the family groups that were ancestrally empowered to exercise local leadership, a clear indication that they were regarded more as project implementers than local leaders (Hohe 2004, 52). The real leaders occupied other positions of authority in the *suku*, including the position of *chefe de suco* and *chefe d'aldeia* and other non-elected customary leadership roles. The Village Development Councils could not compete with the authority exercised by these other leaders – particularly the *chefe de suco* – a problem that manifested in various ways. Sometimes the Village Development Council and *chefe de suco* worked quite well together, but community members would not attend council meetings unless the *chefe de suco* called them in (Ospina and Hohe 2001, 127). Other times, there was direct conflict between Village Development Councils and the *chefe de suco*, as the *chefe de suco* felt excluded and undermined by the council's power to disburse much-needed resources within the village (Hohe 2004, 50–51; Ospina and Hohe 2001, 128).

While the CEP had succeeded in getting resources out to the villages, its primary aim of introducing democratic institutions at the local level was a failure. An underlying flaw within CEP was the inherent tension between speedy resource distribution and the creation of institutional structures designed to encourage local-level democratisation. By privileging the distribution of resources, often according to World Bank priority areas, the CEP allowed insufficient time and care for the encouragement of genuine local participation (Ospina and Hohe 2001).

As UNTAET's administration was to draw to a close on 20 May 2002, the administration focused much of its attention on organising two major elections, the successful conduct of which was to showcase the success of the mission. The first election was for a Constituent Assembly (CA) and was conducted on 30 August 2001. The CA's main task was to write the constitution for Timor-Leste, but through majority CA vote they then went on to become the first Legislative Assembly for independent Timor-Leste. The second election was for the President, held on 14 April 2002. However, despite UN claims that the elections were 'free and fair', there were serious concerns expressed over the legitimacy of the CA election in particular, with one survey conducted at the time indicating that only 5 per cent understood the true

The making of political hybridity 37

purpose of the election, with 61 per cent of respondents wrongly thinking that the election was for the presidency (The Asia Foundation 2001, 4). While these results were alarming to say the least, they were not acted on as neither UNTAET nor CNRT President Kay Rala "Xanana" Gusmão believed the data (Federer 2005, 97).

In addition to the lack of civic education, Hohe (2002) argued that candidates' campaigning for the election was deliberately designed to mislead and manipulate. Their cynical use of traditional and cultural symbolism, now deeply entwined with the successful Timorese resistance to Indonesian occupation, meant that these democratic elections were better labelled a 'totem poll', in which 'voters expressed their honour and respect towards their history and cultural values' (Hohe 2002, 83). Different parties were able to draw on different aspects of Timorese history and culture. Fretilin were still popularly viewed as the resistance front rather than a political party, so they focused on their role in the resistance and encouraged people to express their gratitude to those who had died in the struggle by voting for their party (Hohe 2002, 76). Two new political parties, *Partido Democratico* (PD) and *Partido Social Democratica* (PSD), had been formed out of disenchantment with Fretilin politics, and were comprised of younger Indonesian-speaking activists and intellectuals (Saldanha 2008, 74). These two parties emphasised their role in the clandestine and student resistance movement, often using their code names as a centrepiece for their campaigns (Hohe 2002, 76). More traditionalist parties *Klibur Oan Timor Asuain* (KOTA) and *Partido Povo Timor* (PPT) focused on more localised traditional ideas and symbology, emphasising the continuing importance of the *liurai* within Timor-Leste (Hohe 2002, 77). The manipulation did not stop at the cynical use of symbology – one candidate went so far as to claim he was 'a relative of Prince Charles of England and a major shareholder in the World Bank' (Federer 2005, 100). Not only was this candidate not disqualified, he was subsequently elected to the CA and later went on to become a member of the first Legislative Assembly of Timor-Leste.

It was no surprise to anyone that Fretilin went on to win the majority of votes, winning 43 seats in the national election (representing 57.3 per cent of the vote) and all of the 13 district seats – giving it a total of 56 seats out of 88. The closest rivals were new political parties PD with seven seats and PSD with six seats, both of which appealed to the younger Indonesian-speaking generation. Also predictably, Gusmão, the leader of the resistance movement and hero of independence, was elected as president by an overwhelming majority of 83 per cent. Aware of his popularity and cynical of party politics, Gusmão refused to be affiliated with any one political party.

However, because of the political manipulation and the lack of civic education that surrounded the elections, Hohe dismissed the CA election results as 'reflect[ing] the will of a small elite, the diaspora and overseas-educated individuals who knew how to exploit local beliefs' (2002, 83). While the UN declared the elections a resounding success, conducted as they were with a high voter turnout of 91.3 per cent and without a single violent incident reported, these other factors reveal a more complex story. In the rush to independence, the majority of the population were left behind as the state apparatus for Timor-Leste was being built around them, with insufficient time to lay the foundations for a meaningful democracy. The efforts that had been made through the CEP to establish the foundations for local-level governance were undermined by lack of coordination and lack of local legitimacy. Meanwhile, UNTAET retained their focus on building a cheaper, centralised structure, despite their open acknowledgment that this was probably not what the Timorese people ultimately wanted.

As numerous commentators have argued, many of these issues could have been avoided if UNTAET had been established over a longer timeframe. This, however, required political will within the UN to spend the time and money to do the job properly – political will that was simply not available, particularly when we consider that UNTAET was comparatively one of the more expensive international interventions per capita that the UN has carried out. Instead, the national political apparatus was hastily constructed in such a manner that the majority of people in the rural areas were excluded as the elites engaged in the business of politics. The result, as Hohe described it, was 'a young nation with the appearance of national democratic institutions but unstable at the grassroots' (2004, 44).

On 20 May 2002, in a celebration that was attended by many international dignitaries but which paradoxically – and perhaps symbolically – shut out most ordinary Timorese, UNTAET's administration ended and the independence of Timor-Leste was finally restored. The administrative structure that UNTAET handed to the new Timorese government was highly centralist, and there was much concern expressed at what this meant for the nation. In response, experts recommended greater devolution to the local level to capitalise on the strong ties within communities. These recommendations were ignored by the then Fretilin government, which instead tightened central control over local governance (da Costa Guterres 2006, 234).

By 2006, Timor-Leste was held up as an exemplar of UN state-building efforts (Berger 2006, 6). However, this belief in the 'successful East Timor mission' was shaken when political-military violence broke out in 2006–2007, highlighting the many unresolved issues, including divided leadership, that UN state-building had effectively painted over. This violence, commonly referred to as 'the Crisis', initially played out between those from the east of Timor-Leste, and those from the west, based on popular perceptions of how much the different 'sides' had contributed to independence. But it quickly splintered into complex lines of conflict between different martial arts groups and gangs, with varying allegiance to different political leaders, betraying the many-layered nature of the conflict (Scambary 2009).

In terms of state–society relations, there continues to be a major 'gap' between government decision-makers and the majority of the population who live in the villages, with attendant issues of political and economic disenfranchisement which have been difficult for the Timorese government to deal with. According to the constitution, the government is required to implement decentralisation. Nevertheless, since independent government was restored there have been at least three major iterations of decentralisation policies and laws that have been developed – none of which have been fully implemented. The difficulty in obtaining sufficient political support to implement decentralisation is not terribly surprising, given the centralist government structures which were handed to the Timorese in 2002, and the tendency of power structures to continue to reproduce themselves. It is rare to find a centralist government apparatus willing to give up power to lower levels of government.

At the village level, the *suku* council was formally established in 2004, allowing villagers to directly elect their community representatives and encouraging greater representation for women and young people through a formalised quota system, but also providing space for the ongoing role of customary authorities within the *suku*. However, while council members are important figures locally, they are not part of the government structure and have very limited power to influence how government programmes are carried out in the villages. The role and powers of the *suku* council continues to be an ongoing issue, with the government considering further revision of their status, roles and responsibilities. Also at the local level, there have been various efforts by the Timorese government to bring infrastructural development to the villages through decentralised development programmes. There have been a number of these programmes over the past decade, which have impacted on village life and politics in different ways.

These various political interventions into village life have often not been well-coordinated, and there has certainly been minimal coordination between government programs and the activities of different UN agencies and various non-governmental organisations (NGOs) operating at the local level, which has left much of the responsibility for coordination with the *suku* council. These issues of coordination, together with the complicated politics that arise as liberal democratic institutions are introduced to communities where people live mainly according to *lisan*, means that democracy and independence are having significant and sometimes surprising impacts in local communities, as people explore different ways of being. The influence of political parties is strong, as is that of assorted patron–client and other networks. Local leaders speak increasingly of a breakdown in their authority, particularly in relation to their influence over young people, and new problems are emerging that existing institutions are struggling to contain. Nonetheless, there are many communities that are working hard to solve these problems in creative ways, adapting and integrating new and old forms of legitimacy in an effort to respond to their changing circumstances.

Notes

1 Personal interview with elder, 21 October 2008, *suku* Uma Ana Icu, subdistrict Venilale (district Baucau).

2 Revolution on 25 April 1974 in Portugal overthrowing the fascist *Estado Novo* (New State) regime by non-violent military coup. Named the 'Carnation Revolution' because the soldiers were joined in the streets by many people carrying red carnations to celebrate the end of the regime.
3 Personal interview with community member, 4 November 2008, *suku* Fatulia, sub-district Venilale (district Baucau).

References

The Asia Foundation 2001. *East Timor National Survey of Voter Knowledge (Preliminary Findings)*, The Asia Foundation, Dili.
Beauvais, J.C. 2000. 'Benevolent Despotism: A Critique of UN State-Building in East Timor', *New York University Journal of International Law and Politics*, vol. 33, pp. 1101–1178.
Berger, M. 2006. 'From Nation-Building to State-Building: The Geopolitics of Development, the Nation-State System and the Changing Global Order', *Third World Quarterly*, vol. 27, no. 1, pp. 5–25.
Boxer, C.R. 1947. *The Topasses of Timor*, Indisch Instituut, Amsterdam.
Boxer, C.R. 1960. 'Portuguese Timor: A Rough Island Story: 1515–1960', *History Today*, vol. 10, pp. 349–355.
Budiardjo, C. and Liong, L.S. 1984. *The War Against East Timor*, Zed Books, London.
Capell, A. 1944. 'Peoples and Languages of Timor', *Oceania*, vol. 14, pp. 191–219.
CAVR 2006a. *Chega! The Final Report of the Commission for Reception, Truth and Reconciliation in Timor-Leste (Part 3: The History of the Conflict)*, Commission for Reception, Truth and Reconciliation in Timor-Leste, Dili.
CAVR 2006b. *Chega! The Final Report of the Commission for Reception, Truth and Reconciliation in Timor-Leste (Plain Guide)*, Commission for Reception, Truth and Reconciliation in Timor-Leste, Dili.
Chopra, J. 2003. 'Building State Failure in East Timor', *Development and Change*, vol. 33, pp. 979–1000.
Chopra, J. and Hohe, T. 2004. 'Participatory Intervention', *Global Governance*, vol. 10, pp. 289–306.
da Costa Guterres, F. 2006. *Elites and Prospects of Democracy in East Timor*. PhD thesis published January 2006, Griffith University, Brisbane.
Davidson, K. 1994. *The Portuguese Consolidation of Timor: The Final Stage, 1850–1912*. Unpublished PhD thesis, University of New South Wales, Sydney.
Dunn, J. 1983. *Timor: A People Betrayed*, Jacaranda Press, Milton.
Dunn, J. 2003. *East Timor: A Rough Passage To Independence*, Longueville Media, Double Bay.
Farram, S. 1999. 'The Two Timors: The Partitioning of Timor by the Portuguese and the Dutch', *Studies in Languages and Cultures of East Timor*, vol. 2, pp. 38–54.
Farram, S. 2004. *From 'Timor Koepang' to 'Timor NTT': A Political History of West Timor, 1901–1967*. Unpublished PhD thesis, Charles Darwin University, Darwin.
Federer, J. 2005. *The UN in East Timor: Building Timor Leste, A Fragile State*, Charles Darwin University Press, Darwin.
Fernandes, C. 2004. *Reluctant Saviour: Australia, Indonesia and the independence of East Timor*, Scribe, Melbourne.
Forman, S. 1977. 'East Timor: Exchange and Political Hierarchy at the Timor of the European Discoveries'. In Hutterer, K. (Ed.) *Economic Exchange and Social*

Interaction in Southeast Asia, Papers on South and Southeast Asia No. 13, University of Michigan, Michigan, pp. 97–112.

Forman, S. 1980. 'Descent, Alliance and Exchange Ideology among the Makassae of East Timor'. In Fox, J. (Ed.) *The Flow of Life: Essays on Eastern Indonesia*. Harvard University Press, Cambridge, MA.

Fox, J. 1982. 'The Great Lord Rests at the Centre: The Paradox of Powerlessness in European-Timorese Relations', *Canberra Anthropology*, vol. 5, pp. 22–33.

Gunn, G.C. and Huang, R. 2006. *New Nation: United Nations Peace-Building in East Timor*, self-published, G.C. Gunn.

Gunter, J. 2007. 'Communal Conflict in Viqueque and the "Charged" History of '59', *The Asia Pacific Journal of Anthropology*, vol. 8, pp. 27–44.

Gusmão, K.R., Niner, S., Noronha, A. and Botelheiro, J.L.P. 2000. *To Resist Is To Win! The Autobiography of Xanana Gusmão With Selected Letters and Speeches*, Aurora Books with David Lovell Publishing, Richmond.

Hägerdal, H. 2009. 'The Exile of the Liurai: A Historiographical Case Study from Timor'. In Hägerdal, H. (Ed.) *Responding to the West: Essays on Colonial Domination and Asian Agency*, Amsterdam University Press, Amsterdam.

Hicks, D. 1972. 'Timor-Roti'. In Lebar, F. (Ed.) *Ethnic Groups of Insular Southeast Asia Vol 1: Indonesia, Andaman Islands and Madagascar*, Human Relations Area Files Press, New Haven, pp. 97–105.

Hicks, D. 1983. 'Unachieved Syncretism: The Local-Level Political System in Portuguese Timor, 1966–1967', *Anthropos*, vol. 78, pp. 17–40.

Hohe, T. 2002. 'Totem Polls: Indigenous Concepts and Free and Fair Elections in East Timor', *International Peacekeeping*, vol. 9, pp. 69–88.

Hohe, T. 2004. 'Local Governance After Conflict: Community Empowerment in East Timor', *Journal of Peacebuilding and Development*, vol. 1, pp. 45–56.

King's College 2003. *A Review of Peace Operations: A Case for Change, East Timor*, King's College of the University of London, London.

McWilliam, A. 2005. 'Houses of Resistance in East Timor: Structuring Sociality in the New Nation', *Anthropological Forum*, vol. 15, pp. 27–44.

Moxham, B. 2005. 'The World Bank's Land of Kiosks: Community Driven Development in Timor-Leste', *Development in Practice*, vol. 15, pp. 522–528.

Mubyarto, L.S., Loekman Soetrisno, E., Djatmiko Hudiyanto, I. and Mawarni, S.A. 1991. *East Timor: The Impact of Integration. An Indonesian Socio-Anthropological Study*, Gadja Mada University Research Centre for Village and Regional Development, Jogyakarta; Indonesia Resources and Information Program, Northcote, Australia.

Nicol, B. 2002. *Timor: A Nation Reborn*, Equinox Publishing, Jakarta.

Ospina, S. and Hohe, T. 2001. *Traditional Power Structures and the Community Empowerment and Local Governance Project: Final Report*, UNTAET and World Bank, Dili.

Ramos-Horta, J. 1987. *Funu: The Unfinished Saga of East Timor*, The Red Sea Press, New Jersey.

Rawski, F. 2002. 'Truth-Seeking and Local Histories in East Timor', *Asia-Pacific Journal on Human Rights and the Law*, vol. 3, pp. 77–96.

Rodrigues, R. 2003. 'Introductory Remarks and Keynote Address: There is No Success Without Shared Responsibility'. In de Rham-Azimi, N., Chang, L.L. and Kenky JO, N.K.M. (Eds) *The United Nations Transitional Administration in East Timor (UNTAET): Debriefing and Lessons: Report of the 2002 Tokyo Conference*, Martinus Nijhoff Publishing, Tokyo.

Russell, T. 2008. *Institution Building Problems in East Timor, 1999–2002*. PhD thesis published June 2008, Deakin University, Melbourne.

Saldanha, J. 1994. *The Political Economy of East Timor Development*, Pustaka Sinar Harapan, Jakarta.

Saldanha, J. 2008. 'Anatomy of Political Parties in Timor-Leste'. In Rich, R., Hambly, L. and Morgan, M. (Eds) *Political Parties in the Pacific Islands*, ANU E-Press, Canberra, pp. 69–82.

Scambary, J. 2009. 'Anatomy of a Conflict: The 2006–2007 Communal Violence in East Timor', *Conflict, Security and Development*, vol. 9, pp. 265–288.

Sherlock, K. 1983. *East Timor: Liurais and Chefes de Suco: Indigenous Authorities in 1952*, unpublished evaluation of indigenous political units in Portuguese Timor in the mid-twentieth century, Darwin.

Taylor, J.G. 1999. *East Timor: The Price of Freedom*, Zed Books, London.

Traube, E.G. 1987. *Cosmology and Social Life: Ritual Exchange Among the Mambai of East Timor*, University of Chicago Press, Chicago.

3 Democratisation

Whether we realise it or not, our 'common-sense' understandings of modern law and democracy are built on political theories of institutionalism. According to classic institutionalist theory, institutions comprise the 'rules of the game' for a society. These include the country's laws and regulations, as well as the political, economic and social configurations of a society. The main contribution that institutionalists have made to political and legal theory has been to provide a framework for analysing what impact laws and regulations have on shaping a society and in directing societal change. Institutional theory is very broad and used for many different purposes, and there is much internal contestation between the different strands of contemporary institutionalism, known as 'new institutionalism' (see for example DiMaggio and Powell 1991; Hall and Taylor 1998; North 1991). Institutional theory's claim to explaining the relationship between different sectors of a society has been extremely influential; it was the work of Douglass North (1991) and his focus on the relationship between political institutions and economic development that led to the contemporary theories of good governance that now guide international interventions.

However, these political theories describing the institutions of the modern state have not served well in recognising the importance of customary governance. At best, customary institutions tend to be categorised as 'informal institutions', a residual category which also includes various customs, traditions, sanctions, taboos and societal codes of conduct, and which are contrasted with the 'formal institutions' of state-based law and constitutionalism (see for example North 1991). While this definition is perhaps a step up from their predecessors, known as 'old' institutionalists, who did not recognise customary governance at all, such anaemic descriptions of customary governance as 'informal' fail to reflect the continuing reality for many people across the world.

As can be seen when we examine Timorese history, customary institutions are highly formal in character, and significantly more than a 'resource bank' for state-based institutions to draw upon. The formal character of customary institutions can be clearly seen in practice if one changes the question of 'what are the governance structures in place?' to 'how are people actually governed?'.

For most people in Timorese communities (and many other communities in postcolonial states) customary governance forms their primary source of governance, law and authority (see for example The Asia Foundation 2013b, 21). For them, the institutions of the state are of secondary importance.

The failure to recognise customary institutional structures as deeply formal in character can be put down to a failure of perspective in which, as constitutional theorist James Tully (1995, 41) insightfully notes, the very language of political theory makes it difficult to look beyond the overarching institutions of the state. Institutionalist theories tend to be created from the perspective of those outside looking in – the academics and the policy-makers. Within these theories, the categorisation of customary institutional structures as informal, and state-based institutional structures as formal, ties in with already existing political categorisations that explain particular relationships and interactions. It makes sense to them, and fits into a broader whole. However, while this approach may be useful to explicate particular problems from the perspective of the state, this conventional dividing up of reality fails to adequately reflect the reality of power and authority as it is experienced from within a Timorese *suku*, by community members themselves. A new framework is needed – one which takes into account alternative perspectives.

The reality is that across the villages of Timor-Leste, *lisan* commands great legitimacy. It is central to people's lives, it places them in relation to their land, environment and ancestors, and defines in a very real way who they are as a community and as a people. While *lisan* should not be romanticised, particularly in situations where it reproduces inequalities and injustices relating to class and gender, it is nonetheless central to Timorese identity. Attempting to define *lisan* is a complex philosophical question, as it belongs to a distinct worldview, in which law, spirituality, ethics and ecology overlap (Forman 1980, 153). Timorese customary governance includes, but is not limited to: the important role of traditional authorities in resolving local-level disputes – also guiding how communities are structured (who is in, and who is out); the exchange obligations that underlie a person's existence from birth to death; the complex relationships and mutual obligations that exist between different family groups; the allocation of leadership and decision-making power; the sharing and protection of communal resources; the correct planting and harvesting of crops; and many other areas besides.

The ongoing importance of *lisan*, particularly in the rural areas, has been noted by a number of commentators and is well-recognised as an important facet of contemporary Timorese political, social and spiritual life (Hohe and Nixon 2003; McWilliam 2005; Ospina and Hohe 2001; Trinidade 2008). *Lisan* is sacred, an expression of culture and worldview. It connects individuals to their ancestors, and through the *uma lisan* places them within their extended family network. The importance of custom and ritual, and the need to recognise and serve the ancestors, should never be underestimated within Timorese communities. *Lisan* is not merely an alternative form of governance or dispute resolution: it emanates from a different worldview that acknowledges the continuing presence of the ancestors within Timorese daily life. Everyone knows their *uma lisan*, and knows where they fit in their family structure and in relation to others. Over the years that I have lived and worked in Timor-Leste, everyone I ask, from teenage girls to elderly men, reply that *lisan* and their *uma lisan* is important to them and must be maintained – indeed, more often than not there is confusion or embarrassment that I would ask such stupid questions about principles that to them are so basic.

Within this worldview, the principle of maintaining communal balance through exchange is fundamental. The material world that is inhabited by living things, and the cosmos that is inhabited by the spirit and ancestors, must be kept in balance through rituals of exchange. Failure to observe these rituals leads to imbalance, which can have serious negative consequences such as the spread of disease, harvest failure or natural disasters such as earthquakes (Babo-Soares 2004; Traube 1987). Because of its centrality, Shepard Forman describes the principle of exchange for the Timorese people as 'the idiom of life, symbolically, ideologically and pragmatically' (1980, 153). This idiom is given expression throughout a person's life but is particularly apparent in the important rituals and exchange obligations surrounding marriage and death. The principle of exchange is also a central aspect of customary dispute resolution (Mearns 2007, 48–49).

The exchange relationships that are established within *aldeia* and bind the community together have multiple layers of significance regulating spiritual, ecological, economic and political life. For most people, these relationships form the fundamental source of their wellbeing. While my various discussions with *lia-na'in*[1] emphasise that these layers of significance are inseparable within the customary worldview, it is also clear that there is significant overlap between the political dimensions of customary governance and state-based governance, as both have been established to regulate the same areas of communal life, but in different ways. One of the most important areas of overlap lies in different socio-political ideas of legitimacy for local leadership, which is examined in the next chapter.

Despite its central importance to communities, various commentators during the United Nations (UN) interregnum critically noted that the focus of institution-building and democratisation failed to take *lisan* into account (see for example Chopra 2003; Hohe 2002). Rather, the UN's focus was on democratisation following a blue-printed, Westernised model, culminating in formal, liberal democratic institutions which involved Timorese elites, but which failed to carry the majority of the population with them. As a result, this process of democratic state-building was thin, leaving many people disenfranchised. This has provided the context for state-building since the restoration of independence in 2002, in which government continues to be strongly characterised by centralist decision-making, and politics is dominated by the different political parties that form the main avenue for popular participation. This focus on political parties has in turn been experienced by many communities as divisive, and affiliations to particular political parties have at times been a flash-point for violence (see for example Boavida dos Santos and da Silva 2012, 211–214).

46 Democratisation

This failure to take *lisan* into account, however, was not reflected in the United Nations Transitional Administration for East Timor's (UNTAET) assessment of their impact, as their success or failure was measured by entirely different considerations, the most important of which was the conduct of free and fair elections (Chopra and Hohe 2004). When the Timor-Leste Constituent Assembly was elected and then went on to form government, this was considered sufficient proof of the mission's success – despite many voters' confusion of what they were, in fact, voting for (The Asia Foundation 2001).

From the perspective of many community members, however, the disproportionate influence that was given by the UN to the returned diaspora, and their pragmatic preference for engaging in Portuguese or English which tended to shut out most ordinary Timorese, together with the emphasis on building a new 'modern' state which embodied Western-style democracy, heightened the feeling that key decision-makers did not fully respect the place of tradition and custom – with its many positive elements. This point was forcefully argued by an elder in Venilale who had served as a bureaucrat and important local leader during the latter days of Portuguese rule and throughout Indonesian occupation, and who felt keenly the failure of state-building to recognise customary forms of political participation. As he put it:

> If we *nahe biti boot*[2] inside the house, we put there tobacco and betel nut and we chew and smoke and talk until it is over. Everyone has to talk. There is not one person silent. I am used to this. This is democracy. This democracy is much better than the democracy we copied from foreign countries ... The democracy that we did in 2001, we chose the Members of the Parliament for the Constitution [the Constituent Assembly]. Everyone raised their hands, and followed ... the ones [Timorese diaspora] that came from Mozambique ... We closed our eyes and we supported them but we knew that this was wrong for our country. Why is it that before we were under the Portuguese foreigner and it wasn't good, under the Indonesians and it wasn't good. Now we want independence. Why don't we use the democratic system from before?[3]

Statements such as these are commonly held and there is a deep sense of sadness in these people as they see their state being 'built' around them, with little attention paid to their rights and obligations according to *lisan*. This sadness is generally expressed together with an overall sense of injustice and exclusion, as unemployment rates remain extremely high, poverty is widespread and in some areas deepening, and there continues to be a wide 'gap' between the highly centralised government in Dili, where a small minority are reaping the rewards of development, and the majority of the population remain in poverty in the rural areas. For many people who are unable to see any real improvements in their lives, and for whom daily life is a struggle, there are many questions about who this 'new democracy' is really serving.

Such questions, however, should not be taken as a rejection of democratic ideals. To the contrary: the Timorese people have actively embraced elections, and are very clear that they fought for democracy as well as independence from Indonesian occupation. In fact, if one examines closely the student activist movement for Timorese independence – particularly those students who were studying in Indonesia – it was closely linked to the internal Indonesian struggle for democracy. For many of the activists at the time, the Timorese claim to independence and Indonesian claim for a real democracy was one and the same movement. Questions and comments such as that made by the elder quoted above do not indicate a rejection of democracy. Rather, they indicate a keen interest in building a *deeper* democracy, using as a foundation the positive aspects of local Timorese culture that already exist.

This was perhaps best expressed by this same elder's son – one of the next generation of Timorese leaders – who stated a clear preference for decisions being made by the law, instead of customary authorities. Nonetheless, as he went on to explain, the pursuit of democracy and the rule of law does not mean abandoning the central aspects of *lisan*. As with every other Timorese person I have spoken to, he was of the view that both modern and traditional worldviews were important and have their place – that they can and should 'walk together'. It was not a case of replacing one with the other; in fact, according to his view, the wisdom of *lisan* needed to be protected and preserved:

> The fundamental part of our culture is our relations, our genealogy. We should keep this [knowledge], that we come from our ancestors. So far we don't have any written stories but we only have an oral tradition; we need to transform it into some descriptive stories in order for us to know that we come from which group, which community ... Our *uma lisan*, we need to keep. Maybe our belief in our ancestors, the spirit world we had before we heard about God – these are the basic things that can bring us into a bigger picture of God, so that also we need to keep.[4]

In contemporary Timor-Leste, while *lisan* is central to people's understandings of themselves and how they should relate to each other, so too are modern ideas of democracy. These ideas are often not fully formed, and beyond the advent of regular elections there are many different ideas with varying levels of sophistication surrounding what democracy means, and what it should provide. However, it is central to Timorese identity. For most people, their emergence from colonial rule and the long struggle for independence is intimately tied up with their conception of themselves now as an independent, democratic nation. As one *lia-na'in* explained, democracy cannot be seen as cancelling out the importance of *lisan*. As he put it, 'democracy and the right to self-rule is what people fought for. But the power of *lisan* and connection to the ancestors is what holds communities together, it is central to our [Timorese] identity'.[5]

There are many possible reasons why customary governance has not been integrated into state-building efforts since the vote for independence, and it is likely that there are as many different answers to this question as there were people involved at the time. For some, they simply dismissed customary governance as a thing of the past, and were keen to forge a new path based clearly on modern ideas of democracy and human rights. For others, they saw customary governance as a source of injustice, particularly as it related to inequalities of gender, class and age, and were concerned about propping up these inequalities by giving any recognition to customary leaders. For yet others, they were keen to pursue a single vision of Timorese nationhood, and saw the many different local customary identities as a threat to this vision.

But even for those who were and are sympathetic to the argument that customary governance should somehow be incorporated into state-building efforts, there is no clear methodology to help them do this. A glance through the relevant literature on democratisation and state-building shows that while it is simple enough to find critiques of 'cookie cutter models' of democratisation, it is much harder to find clear, alternative approaches providing practical solutions for policy-makers accustomed to working within the epistemological confines of institutional theory.

At issue, therefore, is a general inability of liberal democratic theory to recognise and incorporate pre-existing forms of customary governance *as part of the process of democratisation*. Much of this comes back to the inherent problems in attempting to define democracy. While the existing books on what democracy is and is not are enough to fill an entire library, democracy and democratisation continue to form a class of ideas that are known to philosophers as 'essentially contested concepts' (Gallie 1956, 168). That is, they are terms for which there is no single clear definition that can be understood as the correct or standard use. Much of the ambiguity comes back to the question of whether democracy should be understood substantively or procedurally, in which substantive democracy is intimately connected with forms of social justice, and procedural democracy focuses on the participation of all eligible citizens in the political process through free and fair elections (Case 2002, 5). When we examine the UN's state-building approach and UNTAET's overall mandate, it is clear that they were expected to follow a procedural approach.

However, the reason that democracy is considered an 'essentially contested concept' is that both definitions are partially correct, and while they have different theoretical foci, they are in practice heavily interdependent. A procedural focus on democracy and democratisation does not focus on elections for its own sake. As well as the inherent good in having a system which allows for the regular, popular change over of leadership, it is based on the presumption that important institutions such as electoral mechanisms are a necessary foundation for the values which are embraced by substantive democracy. Equally, promoters of substantive democracy are at pains to point out that procedural democracy is important but can only take you so far. The idea is that an electoral institution formed on the basis of one person-one vote represents equality in a powerful way, but if it fails to lead to equal treatment between citizens of different class, ethnic groups, genders and other identities, the democracy that results is thin at best.

But this is where it gets confusing. While a functioning democracy may require both substantive and procedural elements, important questions remain. How do they interrelate and is there a hierarchy between them? In a context of limited resources, which facet should be implemented and encouraged first – and how? And, more directly related to the focus of this book, how is the continuing operation of customary governance to be understood where democratisation is being pursued? These are all questions that the literature on state-building and democratisation have tackled, but to which few clear answers have been found.

Democracy or democrazy?

In theory at least, democracy can take many different forms. It can be oriented more towards procedural or substantive approaches; it can clearly embrace a Westernised institutional character, or it can look quite different, emerging more organically from the cultural context in which it is embedded. Nevertheless, the common practice of institutional transfer automatically brings in a certain bias which smuggles in the values of liberalism together with democracy. If you flick through various development agencies' reports on the various successes or failures of democratisation in a given country, the term 'liberal democracy' is commonly used interchangeably with 'democracy' without interrogating the difference between the two. However, liberalism and democracy are in fact distinct political traditions. Democracy can be traced back to ancient Athens in the fifth century BC, in which all free male Athenian citizens had the right to directly participate in political affairs. By contrast, liberalism is a much younger political tradition, going back to the late seventeenth century when John Locke published *Two Treatises of Government* (1689). While democracy traditionally puts the rights of the majority first, liberalism focuses on the rights of the individual. When these two political ideas are combined in a liberal democracy, the idea is that they will balance each other out, ensuring people's right to politically participate and simultaneously guarding individuals against the tyranny of the majority.

The bundling of liberalism and individualism into the 'new' democracy, without taking the time to properly integrate and articulate these norms into people's lived experience, has led, in the case of Timor-Leste, to many local perceptions of modern democracy being characterised by conflict – as opposed to *lisan*, which is aimed at promoting communal cohesion. Local leaders across Timor-Leste have often commented to me that a lack of emphasis on the responsibilities within a democracy has had a particularly negative effect on the young people, contributing to a simplistic elision of democracy with individual (liberal) freedom. These leaders argue that there has been a tendency to conflate the weakening of social control following independence with democracy, resulting in a perception that 'anything goes', an emerging dynamic that was described by the subdistrict administrator in Ainaro as 'democrazy'.[6] On this understanding, state-based and customary governance are posed as opposites, in which dynamic individual freedom is pitted against the principles of communalism and respect that are enshrined within *lisan*. Democratisation is seen to pose an opportunity to fight, to steal, to destroy communal or others' property, or to otherwise act in a way that is detrimental to the community because 'now we are free'. These misinterpretations of democracy, to the detriment of community cohesion, were also commented on by the head *madre* of Venilale, an Italian nun based there since 1988, who said, 'with democracy, they think they can do or say what they want. For them, this is democracy, but when another person says something different, they fight. If you go to a meeting you can't just have one meeting, the people fight really a lot'.[7]

In addition to the introduction of poorly articulated liberal norms and resulting misunderstandings, the procedural focus on elections and competition between political parties has been experienced by many in Timor-Leste as quite divisive. Free competition of political parties is a fairly new phenomenon in Timor-Leste. The first experience of political parties in 1975 resulted in civil war, and during Indonesian occupation the only political parties were the three mandated by the Indonesian government. So it has only been since the restoration of independence that free party-political competition has been a stabilised feature of governance within Timor-Leste, and party politics at every level of government has at times been experienced as an intimidating affair. There has been notable improvement over the past decade, with the most recent national elections in 2012 being largely free of violent conflict. Nonetheless, if we track the process of democratisation in Timor-Leste, the impact of party-political violence in some districts has resulted in localised, ongoing intimidation which centres around political party affiliation. It is not uncommon in some areas for people to be threatened if they fly the 'wrong' party flag, or otherwise are seen to show disrespect to the 'right' political party.

When I first went to live in one of the villages in 2008, I was warned by the parish priest that I should never forget that I was 'living in the mouth of the crocodile' – the party-political violence of the year before meant that conflict lay just under the surface. Only a few months prior, there had been a spate of house-burnings and people held at machete-point because of the outcome of the national elections, as an extremist group of the losing party took the opportunity to violently express their disagreement. In this village, the party politics that had begun with the civil war in 1975 had torn families and communities apart, and these fissures were reopened each time a new issue emerged. As the parish priest went on to explain, 'in 1975 violence came here because of the fighting between different political parties, which created more violence, and many people are traumatised because of this violence. So they imitate the violence, this is the effect of what happened in the past'.[8] As he went on to explain, local leaders who stand to gain from political violence then exploit existing divisions for their own gain: 'these leaders, they are very intelligent, they are very knowledgeable, and they make use of the simple people who have not had education ... these young people are being manipulated and misused, as an instrument of violence'.[9]

The many layers to political violence when it arises mean that it is impossible to trace it back to a single cause. Rather, it has emanated from a range of factors, including ongoing divisions between the Timorese leadership that can be traced through the resistance movement and back to the civil war, the nature of state-building and democratisation with the main focus on conducting elections, lack of civic education, and continuing issues of extreme poverty and structural violence (Galtung 1969) that have not been resolved with independence. The rushed procedural approach that has taken place towards democratisation has meant that while there is often great affiliation expressed by community members to their political party's symbology and flag, there is little understanding of the different policy platforms. This can mean that local political debates centre on affiliation (who is 'in' and who is 'out') rather than the policies and the values that underpin them. These combined factors have effectively worked against other substantive elements of democratisation that promote the values and responsibilities held by citizens within a democracy, making it that much easier for opportunists (including opportunistic representatives of political parties) to exploit existing divisions within Timorese communities.

The speed with which liberal democracy was introduced to the villages has resulted in a clash of values, wherein the young men in particular have used poorly understood liberal principles to shrug off what they see as the oppressive leadership of the local authorities. The local leaders, in turn, are often at a loss to know how to deal with this disrespect, as the old, hierarchical modes of local leadership are no longer sufficient to contain the energies of these frustrated youths. In addition, the procedural focus of democratisation that has privileged political parties without duly considering local impacts on community cohesion, has been experienced in some areas as divisive, reigniting old fracture lines in the community and causing new ones to emerge. None of this is to say that these changes should not be happening. Indeed, despite the potentially divisive impact of political parties at the local level, most people strongly defend their right to be involved in a political party of their choice, as an important route through which they can politically engage. Rather, it throws the spotlight on the *process* of democratisation. What we are looking for is not a false imagining of a static co-existence of 'modern' and 'traditional' structures, but rather a way of understanding the process of negotiation and change as people experience it both within communities and in a broader sense.

A central argument throughout this book is that working with the co-existence of *lisan* and democracy is potentially transformative in Timor-Leste. That is, if the co-existence is properly recognised and harnessed, it can lead to a deepening of values to which the Timorese aspire (including democratic values), and in a manner that respects Timorese identity and culture. But if it is not taken seriously – or worse, is ignored – it can lead to long-term problems that may spread well beyond individual communities. As cannot be emphasised enough, the everyday reality for postcolonial communities is that people simultaneously navigate both customary and state-based governance norms and requirements for legitimacy. It is this reality which must form the basis for policy decisions: however, this does not imply that effectively navigating the co-existence is easy. It is not. There are important paradigmatic differences to be considered, with a broad range of views as to how the specific paradigmatic differences between equality of citizenship and *lisan* should be negotiated. Effectively navigating through these differences in values should be as much a part of Timorese democratisation as the introduction and consolidation of political parties and elections.

Rethinking institutionalism

Because our 'common sense' understandings of law, policy and statehood are based on theories of institutionalism, this is where we need to start in order to understand how customary and state-based governance interact, and what this means in a broader sense. The primary focus of institutional theory is to isolate causal links between institutions and societal change, and in order to do this, institutionalists analytically place one category (formal, state-based institutions) at the centre of analysis and endeavour to explain all other changes in relation to that category. By this analytical device, state-based institutions are placed at the top of the theoretical hierarchy, and other categories are explained in relation to them. This approach to institutionalism is best described as *functionalist*, as it tends to operate on a simplistic cause–effect model, focusing first on the form and content of institutions, and then looking to see the results that they have in shaping individual and communal behaviour. But what if we turn this relationship on its head, taking state-based institutions down from their theoretical pedestal and recognising their co-existence with customary institutions? At its most basic level, recognising the formality of customary institutions means that we also need to adjust institutional theory in order to embrace a messier reality.

There are important reasons to do this. The theories that we use to describe the world can also shape how we see the world. And in turn, how we see the world determines which social arrangements are considered 'relevant' and subject to political analysis, and which are not. When theory and policy adequately reflect people's lived experience, this can help to shape these social interactions and makes the relationship between individuals and the state more coherent. Crucially, however, when theory and policy do not reflect people's realities, this can render specific governance challenges effectively 'invisible' to law and policy-makers.

Up until this point, we have considered the interaction of customary and state-based governance from the 'outside'. As we explored in Chapter 2, the

Portuguese and Indonesian colonisers of Timor-Leste imposed their own systems of governance on communities, which were effectively layered on top of indigenous forms of governance, with varying effects. This was then followed up by the introduction of Westernised systems of governance following the vote for independence, during which time the UN and independent Timorese government embarked on intensive state-building efforts. In their turn, communities have alternately adapted to and/or contested these different imposed structures, but also continued to use their own systems of governance.

This experience as related in Timorese communities is a classic postcolonial governance story, mirrored in different ways across the world, in which external governance structures have been successfully introduced but failed to cancel out pre-existing indigenous forms. But it is also a story of political hybridity told from the outsider's perspective, in which there are two 'types' of governance that co-exist. While the exact boundary between where one layer ends and the other begins is not always clear, this story is one of two distinct layers. There is geographical separation: one is indigenous to the region, and the other emanates from the state centre. And there is ideological separation: one is based on traditional ideas of socio-political legitimacy, and the other is based on liberal democratic ideas of socio-political legitimacy.

However, when we examine closely how things are *actually done* at the local level, governance viewed from within Timorese communities looks very different. When we examine the political reality in Timorese villages, in which both forms of governance co-exist, what becomes apparent is the importance of cross-cutting layers of identity and affiliation. This is the route through which local politics enters, and is also the route through which the requirements of customary and state-based governance are satisfied. For example, as we discuss in the next chapter, it is common for those with customary authority to be democratically elected to the position of village chief. This dual identity means that they are more likely to be able to be considered a legitimate and effective leader. In addition, local dispute resolution often involves a complex interweaving of customary and state-based institutions, with authorities using whatever resources are at hand to help them solve communal problems – sometimes going to the police, other times following customary processes. And economic relationships are particularly complex, with some people actively engaging in the cash economy and others in the subsistence economy. Access to land follows various titling regimes, including customary land tenure and title granted and recognised during Portuguese, Indonesian and independent Timorese government. Important clues on establishing a mode of governance that is true to Timorese identity (instead of forcing an artificial 'choice' between democracy and *lisan*) can be found by examining how villages negotiate the various requirements of both.

The hybrid models of local governance that exist in the *suku* of Timor-Leste have been developed as a natural part of local realities, sometimes as a deliberate strategy to solve recurring problems in the community, other times as a result of the many small, daily decisions that are taken by local leaders when doing their work. A common feature of these different hybrid forms

54 *Democratisation*

is that the relevant question asked by community members is not whether a particular institution falls in the realm of 'customary' or 'state-based' governance, but rather whether it will be an effective and legitimate response to the problem at hand. Sometimes a problem can be solved using either only customary or state-based institutions; other times, it will require the engagement of both. In this way, while customary and state-based governance 'spheres' may be understood to co-exist separately, the many ways in which communities and local leaders navigate both spheres simultaneously is much more fluid and porous.

It is clear that institutional theory and policy cannot be separated from their social context without also missing an important part of the governance puzzle. Nonetheless, functional accounts of institutionalism – upon which classical legal theory rests – fail to provide any real insight into how these fluid dynamics are navigated. According to functional institutionalists, institutions do their work in structuring society by providing a set of rules with which people for various reasons then comply. By this account, institutions are created by the government through laws and regulations, enforced by the police, and the citizens of the state are simply subject to those institutions. In their turn, citizens hold decision-makers to account through various institutions, one of the most important being the advent of regular elections. In situations where the desired outcomes do not follow, a functional approach would simply presume that the model needs work and the institutions need 'strengthening'. This simplistic cause–effect model for understanding institutions fails to recognise how they interact, shift and evolve as a natural part of local politics.

However, if we shift focus away from this emphasis on the desired outcomes to consider the *process* of institutionalisation, new ways of thinking emerge. As we have seen, institutions are not simply impersonal forces to which people are subject, they also form part of the political and social context within which people engage with each other, putting forward certain values and ideologies over others, meeting various needs, solving individual and communal problems, and using and distributing resources. There have been pockets of success in which the Timorese government has succeeded in adapting policy so that it engages with local realities, shifting dynamics to suit both local and national priorities. One such pocket of success can be seen in a local water management programme, in which local groups are formed and customary authorities and land-owners consulted throughout the planning process to ensure water piping projects do not unwittingly desecrate sacred sites.

Another pocket of success involves the experience of political party affiliation on the *suku* council. There have now been two iterations of the law governing the *suku* council, the first passed in 2004 (Decree Law 5/2004) and the second in 2009 (Law 3/2009). While the overall impact of Law 3/2009 is a mixed bag, with some aspects negatively impacting on local governance arrangements, a positive aspect was how political parties were dealt with. When the *suku* council was first created in 2004, the members of the council were elected on the basis of their political parties affiliation. Nevertheless, the divisive impact of political parties interfered with local ways of ensuring local leaders were fit for the job. As an elder and former *xefe suku* in Venilale argued, local leaders' affiliation with political parties had undermined the inherently democratic nature of community elections, where everyone knew the candidates and could make their choices based on their demonstrated ability as local leaders. As he put it:

> Now I compare with when I was *xefe suku* before 1997 ... [in 2004] in order to choose the local leadership we used the symbols of the political parties [on the ballot papers]. To use the flags, and to use the political parties is not good ... In a democracy the symbols of the political parties are used for the presidential and parliamentary elections, that is okay. But to do elections for the *xefe suku* and for the community authorities we should not use the symbols of the political parties.[10]

As he went on to explain, it is more legitimate if community leaders work their way up through the local leadership hierarchy, through family structures, as they gain in experience and win the trust of the community. Prior to the introduction of the party system within *suku* politics, the most important considerations in selecting local leaders were the candidates' place within the community: whether they came from the *liurai* house, their affiliation with family, their experience with local leadership and ability to command respect, and their perceived ability to do the job. This was then undermined with the introduction of political parties, where community authority was no longer based solely on the leaders' position within the community. As a result, lines of authority and accountability were moved away from the family groups as a source of communal cohesion, and national political divisions were driven down to the local level. In the 2009 legislation, *suku* councils were no longer openly affiliated with political parties, a move greeted with approval in a number of districts (The Asia Foundation 2013a).

In a sense, the decision around party-political affiliation on *suku* councils can be considered to have hit a 'sweet spot' in which both national and local priorities were satisfied. There were political reasons for the national government to remove political parties – in particular, the desire to stop the opposition political party, *Frente Revolucion á ria de Timor-Leste Independente* (Fretilin), from claiming greater popularity because they were historically more successful in *suku* council elections. But the decision also satisfied local priorities, in which the greatest demand of local leadership is that they be primarily accountable to the community. Any other affiliation which moves accountability away from the community to other bodies, such as political parties or the government itself, is seen to diminish their legitimacy in the eyes of the community (The Asia Foundation 2013a, 7–8).

How, then, are we to capture these insights to better inform institutionalist theory, and, by association, mainstream approaches to policy-making?

According to critical theorist Robert Cox, institutions form only one aspect of a broader dynamic through which they gain the capacity to influence individuals' behaviour and shape societal outcomes. Institutionalisation, or the process through which institutions 'stick' in society, actually comes about through a complex interplay between three main categories: power, ideas and institutions (Cox 1981, 140). In some situations, institutions that are introduced will stick because they already fit in with existing ideas of legitimacy and conform with existing power dynamics. These are easily incorporated into the local governance environment. But institutions may also fall out of step with ideas or material forces. Formal institutions, if they attempt to push too far ahead of community ideology or existing power relations, may be subverted, or frustrated in their purpose. But this doesn't make them a failure. If sufficient resources (power) are invested by the state to back up the introduction of these new ideas and institutions, they may over time become institutionalised, even if people didn't initially buy into the values that underpinned them. Equally, if the majority of people are convinced of the values that underpin these new institutions at the outset, they may also over time become institutionalised as they influence how power and resources are distributed.

An important thing to remember, however, is that unlike functionalist accounts of institutionalism which presume that an institution will ultimately lead to a static outcome, this way of understanding the process of institutionalisation means it is never absolute. In many cases, the process is actually quite fluid, as the changing ideologies and distribution of material resources and power form an ongoing dialectic with the institutions of the state. As stated earlier, the processes by which institutions do their work in society is significantly more complex – and the claims that law-makers can make regarding the impact that written institutions have in shaping and framing societal outcomes needs to be correspondingly more humble.

To account for the co-existence of customary and state-based governance, and the fluidity of institutionalisation, Figure 3.1 is an adaptation of Cox's (1981, 136) figure, depicting institutionalisation as a fit between ideas, institutions and material capabilities, and incorporating the co-existence of customary and state-based governance.

Moving out attention from outcomes to process, and recognising the co-existence of state-based and customary governance within this dynamic, offers a very different perspective on local-level governance. Through everyday local politics, both state-based and customary institutional structures are strategically engaged by local leaders and community members to fulfil various needs. Many local leaders source their legitimacy through both customary and state-based notions of socio-political legitimacy. Within this broad framework, there is an ongoing dialectic between ideas and material capabilities (resources and power) as they influence – and are influenced by – both customary and state-based governance structures and norms. Neither structure on its own determines outcomes, but they nonetheless have an important

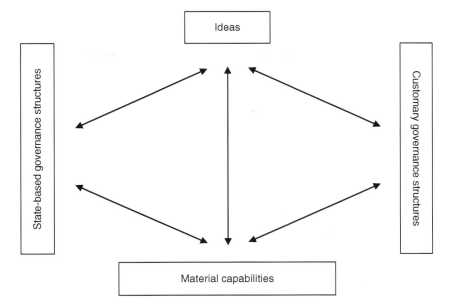

Figure 3.1 The fluidity of institutionalisation.

influence over the reproduction of ideologies and material power within a village, as together they structure social life, imposing pressures and constraints on the life-choices that are available to people. The process of institutionalisation is rarely a simple question of either community 'acceptance' or 'rejection' of state-based institutions. Rather, it is a complex process that is negotiated by the local leaders as they use existing resources to meet community needs, and to pursue individual political agendas.

This is how culture changes. There is now a generational divide across the villages of Timor-Leste, which continues to express itself in different ways. While many of the older generation in the villages experience a sense of loss that certain aspects of *lisan* may be slipping away, the younger generation are more open to change – so long as it is the right type of change and comes at the right pace. As one younger man explained, he dreams of a future Timor-Leste that accords greater weight to modern ideas of democracy and the rule of law, but he and his peers also need to be respectful of the older leaders:

> I don't want something more traditional, I want things to be decided according to the law. But how do you accelerate that? We can kill people's spirits, because some old people who are still with the traditional ways, and we go on with the modern way we can kill them. So does this mean we should wait for them? That needs a lot of discussion.[11]

Going forward

There is no doubt that the past ten years or more have changed the political culture of Timor-Leste – for villagers as well as those in the city. The influence of democratisation is felt in various ways, including the ways in which customary ideas of socio-political legitimacy are creatively interpreted in order to adapt to the new laws of the Timorese government, as well as the potentially damaging effects of poorly-understood liberal norms. It is therefore a mistake to refer to customary governance as though it has remained unchanged and unchanging or is separate from the governance of the state. But neither has customary governance been entirely subsumed within the state. To argue along this line is to over-emphasise the penetration of the state at the local level and ignore the importance that traditional concepts hold for the daily lives of people in the rural areas.

In recognising the co-existence of state-based and customary governance, it is clear that customary governance derives legitimacy in the *suku* of Timor-Leste because it fills important community needs – particularly in the context of limited state capacity to provide for those needs. However, there is danger in an over-dependence of state-based institutions on customary governance. While customary governance continues to exert a strong influence in the *suku* of Timor-Leste, there are important warning signs that it is not equipped to deal with modern influences and challenges that are now entering Timorese communities. The current lack of investment leaves state-legitimised authority figures disempowered and, particularly in aspects of communal life where customary governance does not apply, opens the door for political opportunists who seek to exploit these institutional gaps in the local governance environment.

This offers a very different lens through which to consider the process of democratisation in the villages. As has already been discussed, much of the international development industry's approach is based on the binary of tradition and modernity, and the normative assessment that modernity is to be preferred over tradition. This is what drives theories of progress, development and democratisation, and ultimately keeps the international development industry alive. Perhaps their assessments are correct – at certain times and in certain areas. But close examination of village life shows that people are also making their own normative assessments, choosing ways of working and living which best suit their needs as they see them. They are not merely passively subject to these governance structures, they are actively engaged in these processes. And their normative choices have a decisive impact on how externally-introduced institutions play out in each village. As such, rather than attempting to 'replace' customary institutions with state-based institutions through formalistic interventions, the focus needs to move to recognising the *balance* that is negotiated between customary and state-based governance by villagers themselves – and the impact that this has on different sectors of the community. These dynamics are all intensely political processes that are susceptible to change over time, and form the basic framework through which political change comes about.

These insights into how institutions fit into the governance landscape underline the difficulty for development practitioners in carrying out their work. The development industry is largely mechanistic, driven as it is by donors' demands that programmes be clearly designed to meet defined policy aims. This overall structure tends to result in a reliance on logframes (logical frameworks) that lay out specified outputs and outcomes, and which can blind development practitioners to the importance of process. This is fundamentally at odds with the more humble approach outlined above, recognising that so much is outside policy-makers' control.

This task becomes even more difficult for international development practitioners, as they often do not have a good grasp of local communities, and therefore lack even a basic capacity to predict how new institutions will be accepted and incorporated into the local governance environment. Over the years that I have worked in the development industry, I have seen many examples of well-intentioned policy and legal experts suggesting reforms to hot-button issues such as land, or village boundaries, simply for the sake of bringing it into line with other policy areas. The potential impact that such reforms would have on local understandings of identity, inflaming pre-existing land disputes, were often lost on them, as they focused on their job of streamlining the national legal apparatus. While impact on land, territory and identity is perhaps a more obvious example, the unintended consequences of institutional interventions are littered throughout the history of international development, as resources have been captured and used for purposes for which they were not initially intended, existing lines of conflict have been exacerbated and deepened, and communities continue to wait for the 'benefits' of development.

Notes

1 *Lia-na'in* literally means 'holder of the words'. This is the customary authority figure who holds ritual and judicial power in the community.
2 *Nahe biti boot* is a ritual for dealing with situations that consists of sitting together to discuss. Literally translates as 'laying the big mat on the floor'.
3 Personal interview with elder, 3 November 2008, *suku* Uatu Haco, subdistrict Venilale (district Baucau).
4 Personal interview with community member, 14 September 2008, *suku* Uato Haco, subdistrict Venilale (district Baucau).
5 Personal interview with *lia-na'in*, 20 December 2008, *suku* Ainaro, subdistrict Ainaro (district Ainaro).
6 Personal interview with subdistrict Administrator, 17 December 2008, subdistrict Ainaro (district Ainaro).
7 Personal interview with parish nun, 8 October 2008, subdistrict Venilale (district Baucau).
8 Personal interview with parish priest, 8 July 2008, subdistrict Venilale (district Baucau).
9 Personal interview with parish priest, 8 July 2008, subdistrict Venilale (district Baucau).

10 Personal interview with elder, 30 July 2008, *suku* Uato Haco, subdistrict Venilale (district Baucau).
11 Personal interview with community member, 14 September 2008, *suku* Uato Haco, subdistrict Venilale (district Baucau).

References

The Asia Foundation 2001. *East Timor National Survey of Voter Knowledge (Preliminary Findings)*, The Asia Foundation, Dili.
The Asia Foundation 2013a. *Reflections of Law 3/2009*, The Asia Foundation and Ministry for State Administration, Dili.
The Asia Foundation 2013b. *Law and Justice Survey*, The Asia Foundation, Dili.
Babo-Soares, D. 2004. '*Nahe biti*: The Philosophy and Process of Grassroots Reconciliation (And Justice) in East Timor', *The Asia Pacific Journal of Anthropology*, vol. 5, pp. 15–33.
Boavida dos Santos, A. and da Silva, E. 2012. 'Introduction of a Modern Democratic System and its Impact on Societies in East Timorese Traditional Culture', *Local-Global Journal*, vol. 12, pp. 206–220.
Case, W. 2002. *Politics in Southeast Asia: Democracy or Less*, Curzon Press, Richmond.
Chopra, J. 2003. 'Building State Failure in East Timor', *Development and Change*, vol. 33, pp. 979–1000.
Chopra, J. and Hohe, T. 2004. 'Participatory Intervention', *Global Governance*, vol. 10, pp. 289–306.
Cox, R. 1981. 'Social Forces, States and World Orders: Beyond International Relations Theory', *Millennium: Journal of International Studies*, vol. 10, pp. 126–155.
DiMaggio, P.J. and Powell, W.W. 1991. *The New Institutionalism in Organizational Analysis*, Chicago University Press, Chicago.
Forman, S. 1980. 'Descent, Alliance and Exchange Ideology among the Makassae of East Timor'. In Fox, J. (Ed.) *The Flow of Life: Essays on Eastern Indonesia*, Harvard University Press, Cambridge, MA, pp. 97–112.
Gallie, W.B. 1956. 'Essentially Contested Concepts', *Proceedings of the Aristotelian Society*, vol. 56, London, Harrison & Sons, Ltd, pp. 167–198.
Galtung, J. 1969. 'Violence, Peace and Peace Research', *Journal of Peace Research*, vol. 6, no. 3, pp. 167–191.
Hall, P.A. and Taylor, R.C.R. 1998. 'Political Science and The Three New Institutionalisms'. In Soltan, K., Uslaner, E. and Haufler, V. (Eds) *Institutions and Social Order*, Michigan University Press, Michigan, pp. 15–44.
Hohe, T. 2002. 'The Clash of Paradigms: International Administration and Local Political Legitimacy in East Timor', *Contemporary Southeast Asia*, vol. 24, pp. 569–590.
Hohe, T. and Nixon, R. 2003. *Reconciling Justice: 'Traditional' Law and State Judiciary in East Timor*. Report prepared for the United States Institute of Peace Project on Peacekeeping and the Administration of Justice. January 2003. Available at: www.ids.ac.uk/ids/law/pdfs/hohendixon.pdf.
Locke, J. 1689. *Two Treatises of Government: In the Former, The False Principles, and Foundation of Sir Robert Filmer, and His Followers, Are Detected and Overthrown. The Latter is an Essay Concerning the True Original, Extent, and End of Civil Government*, Awnsham Churchill, London.

McWilliam, A. 2005. 'Houses of Resistance in East Timor: Structuring Sociality in the New Nation', *Anthropological Forum*, vol. 15, pp. 27–44.

Mearns, D. 2007. 'Masking the Pain: Nation Building and Local Anaesthetic in Timor-Leste'. In Shoesmith, D. (Ed.) *The Crisis in Timor-Leste: Understanding the Past, Imagining the Future*, CDU Press, Darwin, pp. 43–51.

North, D. 1991. 'Institutions', *The Journal of Economic Perspectives*, vol. 5, pp. 97–112.

Ospina, S. and Hohe, T. 2001. *Traditional Power Structures and the Community Empowerment and Local Governance Project: Final Report*, UNTAET and World Bank, Dili.

RDTL 2004. *Decree Law 5/2004 on Community Authorities*, Dili, Timor-Leste.

RDTL 2009. *Parliamentary Law 3/2009 on Community Leadership and their Election*, Dili, Timor-Leste.

Traube, E.G. 1987. *Cosmology and Social Life: Ritual Exchange among the Mambai of East Timor*, University of Chicago Press, Chicago.

Trinidade, J. 2008. 'An Ideal State for East Timor: Reconciling the Conflicting Paradigms'. In Mearns, D. and Farram, S. (Eds) *Democratic Governance in Timor Leste: Reconciling the Local and the National*, Charles Darwin University Press, Darwin, pp. 160–188.

Tully, J. 1995. *Strange Multiplicity: Constitutionalism in an Age of Diversity*, Cambridge University Press, New York.

4 Local leadership

Given the complexity of democratic institutions' interaction with customary forms of governance, it is perhaps not surprising that local forms of authority are equally complex. Authority structures are one of the important ways in which hybrid governance is navigated, and gives form and expression to the choices that are made in individual communities in balancing customary and state-based governance norms. In coming to understand how patterns of local leadership are formed, we can also come to understand in more concrete ways how postcolonial governance dynamics are shaped.

As we have seen, *suku* level leadership is perhaps the oldest modality of leadership existing on the island of Timor, playing an important role prior to Portuguese colonisation through to the present day. Given the ongoing importance of *suku* leadership, it was clear in the early days of Timorese independence that a local governing body would need to be created to respond to community concerns and represent them to the Timorese national leadership. Following the vote for independence in 1999, one of the first acts of the Timorese leadership was to establish *suku* and *aldeia* representatives in the villages, mainly comprising those who had headed up the resistance network in that village and who went on to fill the important role of *suku* or *aldeia* chief.

In 2004, the Timorese government then went on to create the *suku* council, thereby continuing the Timorese legacy of village leadership, and formalising existing practices of local authority. There is a *suku* council operating in each of Timor-Leste's 442 *suku*. The *suku* council was first officially created, in its present form, through Decree Law 5/2004, and the election method and council membership was then updated slightly a few years later through Law 3/2009. Council members are directly elected by eligible voting members of the *suku* every six years. The council is headed by the *xefe suku* (chief of the *suku*), who is the most important figure on the council, responsible for fulfilling some of the more demanding competencies under the law. Other members of the council include all of the *xefe aldeia* (chief of the *aldeia*), representing each of the *aldeia* within the *suku*, along with one elder, two women's representatives and two youth representatives – one man, one woman. There is also a *suku lia-na'in*, added to the council in 2009, who is not elected but specially appointed by the council members during their first meeting following election into office. While building on a long history of *suku* leadership, the *suku* council also introduced some important modernising changes – in particular, through the introduction of direct elections and the inclusion of the women and youth representatives. In the original 2004 legislation, each *suku* council member was elected individually. This was changed in 2009 to the *pakote* (package) system, in which candidate *suku* councils are formed prior to election and people vote for their preferred council. While more cost-effective for the electoral agencies, the *pakote* system has not been viewed favourably by community members and leaders, who see it as limiting their capacity to elect the most appropriate person to each post (The Asia Foundation 2013, 7–8).

The *suku* council is itself an interesting institution. While it exercises many functions that might be considered local government responsibilities, it is not officially a government body. Nonetheless, council members are voted in via popular elections which are run by the two official state electoral bodies every six years. Under Law 3/2009, council members are legally defined as 'community authorities', and the council is recognised as 'the collective body which aims to organise the participation of the community in the solution of its own problems, protect its interests and represent it as necessary'. This understanding of the council was confirmed by the Timor-Leste Court of Appeal, which judged *suku* councils to be 'traditional organisational structures',[1] recognised by the law to have certain competencies but not considered local government. The *suku* council's unique legal status indicates the pragmatic decision-making of a centralist government, in which there are limited resources to pay for 442 local government bodies, when the same or similar results can be achieved by defining them as 'traditional'. As the Court of Appeal explained it, because *suku* leadership existed prior to the formation of the Timorese state itself, *suku* councils are best understood as 'intermediate bodies'. Neither government nor community-based organisation, they are in effect their own special category.

Despite the historical and customary roots of the *suku* council, it is very clear that the *suku* council is part of the new, state-based apparatus – albeit with a unique legal status. Research conducted across five different districts in 2013 confirmed that the primary source of legitimacy for *suku* council members was their status as directly elected community representatives, who are primarily accountable to the community (The Asia Foundation 2013, 1). Leaders on the *suku* council operate in tandem with various customary authority figures who continue to be recognised and exercise important local functions. *Lia-na'in* are generally responsible for maintaining *lisan* in the community, leading ceremonies and resolving disputes, among other things. Most extended families have their own *lia-na'in*, and there are also *lia-na'in* who operate at the *aldeia* and *suku* level of governance. In some *aldeia* and *suku*, they may come together to form a council; in others they may operate individually. Customary authority is structured through the hierarchy that exists between the *uma lisan*, and family groups. *Liurai*, or royalty, are those who are empowered by the ancestors to lead the community, assisted by the *datu*, or aristocrats. In addition, there is often another *uma lisan* which is considered more important than the *liurai*'s *uma lisan*, responsible for spiritual concerns and providing checks and balances on the *liurai*'s exercise of authority.

This provides a broad thumbnail sketch of customary authority structures and associated powers at the local level. However, it is also important to note that these arrangements often vary significantly from one clan to the next, reflecting the specific features of the *lisan* and culture of that area. For example, in the enclave of Oekussi, there are the authorities of the *naijuf* (the local king) who acts as the executive organ; the *tobe*, who is responsible for establishing *tarabandu* for agricultural purposes; and finally the *meo*, who is like the police, providing security for the land (Boavida dos Santos and da Silva 2012, 214–215). In Ainaro, there is the *liurai metan* (king of the 'black' *tais*[2]), and the *liurai mutin* (king of the 'white' *tais*), as well as assorted *liana'in* and *xefes*.[3] There are commonalities from one clan to the next, but there are also important differences.

In general, customary authorities are well-respected, and their roles are actively relied on in most communities. Where the *liurai* still exist, they are generally considered as central figures to the community. However, there are also some *suku* that no longer have a *liurai*. This might because they are 'new' *suku*, created during Indonesian or Portuguese colonisation by moving populations without the customary authority structure in place. This is the case, for example, in *suku* Bairo Pite, in the capital city, Dili. As recounted by Timorese academic Mateus Tilman, the people have come to a unique solution to this problem, effectively transferring their loyalty to the customary authority of the traditional kingdom Karaketu Mota Ain, which gives customary protection over them and allows them to implement important ceremonies in the *suku* (Tilman 2012, 201).

It is clear that *lisan* and culture have a central place in contemporary Timorese *suku*. Nonetheless, it is almost impossible to find someone who expresses a wish to return to the days of the *liurai* as was experienced during Portuguese colonisation. Recollections of Portuguese indirect rule, associated *liurai* brutality in some parts and the lack of basic rights for ordinary villagers are still part of living memory for many people. Stories of forced labour and worse, of arbitrary beatings for offences such as not wearing 'proper' clothes, of the hardships associated with the head tax imposed on every male over a certain age, and many other stories besides are still commonly recounted by the elders. As one local activist in Ainaro forcibly argued, while he believes that *lisan* is very important in his village and must be respected as part of Timorese identity, this is quite different to the monarchical rulership of the *liurai* that existed during Portuguese colonisation. The stories of his parents and grandparents have convinced him that Timor-Leste is much better now as an independent, democratic nation. Timorese activism against such misuse of authority is as much a part of the Timorese legacy as the ongoing presence of customary governance: towards the end of Portuguese colonisation in the 1970s, and in response to *liurai* brutality, Timorese activists were standing up against the *liurai* system, pushing for a new system of governance that would embrace social democratic principles.

Taking all of this into account, in the same way that *lisan* and modern law are distinct from each other, in that they emanate from separate worldviews and sources of power, the authority of state-based and customary authorities is also explained by local leaders as two separate spheres of activity. Non-elected customary authorities are well-respected, taking a leadership role in *lisan* festivities, ceremonies, the imposition of customary prohibitions and dispute resolution. However, when questioned, people are clear that these customary authorities cannot exercise political power, which is conferred by the state. By contrast, elected leaders are the community representatives and take a political role in their communities. According to this view, there is a strict division that must be maintained – customary leaders are important people who hold symbolic, cultural and spiritual power, while *suku* council members hold political power. Symbolic, cultural and spiritual authority is conferred via *lisan*; political authority is conferred via election. This means that for customary leaders to also exercise political power, they must engage with the modern state structures. As the *xefe suku* of Ainaro explained:

> In Ainaro there were *liurai* since a long time ago ... they were important, according to the tradition and the culture in Ainaro and it still exists. But now Timor is independent, the people still respect them but use the democratic system, with the right to freedom, for anyone to occupy the post ... [*Liurai*] have an influence in the district ... [But] if they want to influence the government, they can have a [political] party, they can have the mandate of the government ... Almost everything is done through elections, according to majority.[4]

Similar comments were echoed by the *liurai mutin* of Ainaro, who also occupied the post of subdistrict administrator. Traditionally in this area, the *liurai mutin*, or 'king of the white *tais*', was responsible for political decision-making, and subject to the authority of the *liurai metan*, or 'king of the black *tais*', who was responsible for spiritual matters. Nevertheless, as he explained, this was a thing of the past and while he effectively filled the two separate roles of *liurai mutin* and subdistrict administrator, he was also responsible for maintaining them independently of each other:

> I am here not as the *liurai* but as subdistrict administrator ... now Timor is in the era of democracy so there aren't *liurai*. Now there is a new structure, the structure of independence ... The *liurai* can be a representative, but to be responsible or in charge he cannot anymore.[5]

Hybridity of local leadership

While this description of neatly separated spheres of authority clearly outlines how power is divided in a *suku*, it fails to acknowledge that the *liurai mutin* mentioned above is able to carry out his work as subdistrict administrator more effectively and easily *because* he can command respect and trust through his customary role. He is able to claim legitimacy in his role not only because he is an appointee of the government, but also because traditionally the ancestors have conferred this right on him and his bloodline.

Close examination of how authority is conferred and exercised similarly demonstrates that there are aspects of customary and state-based authority that overlap and interact in important ways. For example, the strict compartmentalisation of customary and state-based leadership that is so often described fails to recognise the reality that local leadership roles that are part of the government structure tend to be occupied by people who can claim customary authority. For example, it is very common for elected *xefe suku*, *xefe aldeia* and *lia-na'in* in Timor-Leste to come from the 'right' families that can claim customary legitimacy, and in a number of villages the *xefe suku* is also the traditionally-legitimised *liurai*. This dynamic in which a single individual holds both customary and state-based leadership roles has been noted by many people, including the late resistance veteran and son of a *liurai* house, Virgilio dos Anjos:

> When [the political party] Fretilin talked about bringing down the *liurai* [during the civil war], there was a massive reaction from the people. It was clear that there was a very strong feeling against the *liurai*. But during the war against Indonesia, as it became apparent that many of the children of *liurai* were also struggling for independence, the issue became more confused. And now, we can see that in the villages, most people are electing people of *liurai* families to become the *xefe suku* [village head]. The tradition of the *liurai* is still very strong.
>
> (Grimshaw 2009)

The authority which is exercised by the *liurai* and other customary leaders is viewed with suspicion in some quarters – particularly among those looking to democratise local governing arrangements. As discussed previously, the concern with giving too much power to customary authorities was clearly demonstrated in the World Bank's Community Empowerment Program (CEP), which deliberately excluded their participation in the CEP village councils. This proved to be a key failure in the programme, as young 'smart' people who could not claim customary authority were elected onto the council, and tension emerged between the 'real' (customary) leaders and this new council (Hohe 2004, 50–51; Ospina and Hohe 2001, 128). The CEP came to an end in 2002.

Unlike these councils established through community-driven development programmes, candidature and election to the *suku* council is open to anyone who is able to form a prospective *suku* council and put themselves forward. This has resulted in a strong customary authority presence within the *suku* council, as communities have endeavoured to fulfil customary notions of socio-political legitimacy with the need to find someone who is capable of leading the *suku*. The resulting balance that is found in incorporating customary authority onto the *suku* council varies from one place to the next, depending on the local history and politics of the area. The importance of customary authority also varies significantly according to the role on the *suku* council – whether one is *xefe aldeia*, *xefe suku*, *lia-na'in*, youth representative or women's representative.

The various modalities of hybrid local authority which have emerged are, of course, due to a combination of different factors. At first blush, it is not unreasonable to presume that privilege and power have a tendency to reproduce themselves, as those with access to more resources also have more access to education, more influence with others who also occupy leadership roles, and may have a greater sense of entitlement to occupying leadership positions, together, perhaps, with a greater sense of responsibility in looking after 'their' people. These material, temporal factors apply to all members on the *suku* council, and it is not uncommon to find husbands and wives, brothers and sisters sitting on the same *suku* council.

However, there are also strict customary rules which are applied to some council members, in particular the *xefe suku*, in some *suku*. These rules determine whether or not he or she is eligible to take on the mantle. This is because, in customary terms, the elected role of *xefe suku* also represents a continuation of the customary role of *liurai*. Similar considerations may also apply to *xefe aldeia* and *suku lia-na'in*, again depending on the history and politics of the area. For these officials, three different political models of hybridity have emerged organically within communities, as they look to satisfy both state-based and customary notions of legitimacy. The first two are both 'co-incumbency' models, which can be termed as a strict co-inheritance approach and a 'traditional house candidate' approach. The third is an 'authorisation' model (Cummins and Leach 2012, 98–101).

The two co-incumbency models describe a theme that varies only in the strictness of the approach, in which an individual who can claim customary legitimacy is also elected to the position of *xefe suku*. This means the same individual effectively occupies two different positions. In the first, the hereditary *liurai* is routinely elected as the *xefe suku*, creating an ongoing dynamic in which the *xefe suku* electoral system parallels the hereditary authority of the *liurai* family. This can be seen, for example, in *suku* Uai Oli, in the subdistrict of Venilale, where the *liurai* is expected by his community to stand for the position of *xefe suku*. According to local lore in this *suku*, if the community is not led by the *liurai*, the spiritual balance with the ancestors will be upset and they will become very 'sick'.[6] Fitting into the same co-incumbency model is *suku* Uma Uain Kraik in Viqueque, in which the traditional *liurai* is routinely elected to the position of *xefe suku*.[7] This strict hereditary system appears to

68 *Local leadership*

be relatively rare, however, and may also be changing. In the 2009 elections, the *liurai* of Uai Oli was re-elected with just 48.95 per cent of the vote, narrowly beating another candidate who is related to him, but not immediately in the line of succession, who received 43 per cent.

The second, more common co-incumbency model – the model it appears *suku* Uai Oli may be leaning towards – is the traditional house approach, in which the *xefe suku* is elected from the *liurai's uma lisan*. This opens up the field to a wider range of candidates, allowing for meritocratic competition while also satisfying customary requirements of legitimate local leadership. This dynamic can be found across many different *suku* in Timor-Leste. The incorporation of customary authority into state-based leadership structures can come with sometimes surprising connections. For example, in *suku* Soro, in the subdistrict of Ainaro, the *xefe suku* was one of the few female *xefe suku* voted into office in the 2004/2005 elections.[8] As she explained, as a woman she would have been traditionally required to 'stay in the kitchen', unable to take on the role of *suku* leader. However, customary considerations nonetheless came into play when her political party approached her to stand for election – they viewed her as a good candidate, likely to attract a high number of votes, partly because she came from the *liurai's uma lisan*:

> From our ancestors they say that the biggest *uma lisan* in this *suku* is this one [so] I became *xefe suku* partially because of my *uma lisan* … my family, in terms of the traditional, is the most important in this *suku*. But it was not only because of the culture that I can be *xefe suku*. It is based on my behaviour and the behaviour before, the connection with the community, who the people trust to be *xefe suku*.[9]

The third 'authorisation' model covers the various mechanisms that allow communities to recognise an elected *xefe suku* without customary legitimacy, thus satisfying cultural needs. In some areas, the *liurai* will give the elected *xefe suku* his blessing, allowing him to carry out certain functions (Cummins and Leach 2012, 99–100; Tilman 2012, 200). In rural Oecusse, for example, the *liurai* needs to bless the *xefe suku* before representing him in traditional or ritual ceremonies – otherwise, he will be cursed. In Los Palos, when the *xefe suku* is elected to the position, the *liurai* would grant him permission by passing on the *rota*[10] through a special ceremony, giving the elected *xefe suku* the right to act as his representative. Culturally, it is believed that the *rota* is too 'heavy' for people who are not culturally legitimised.

But customary authority is not the only source of legitimacy, and there are many variations throughout different s*uku*. Once again, dependent on the history, culture and politics of the particular area, different *xefe suku* were able to explain the multiple factors that came into play, beyond their perceived capacity to do the job, when they were voted into office. Some factors were emphasised over others. For some, it was important that they came from the *liurai* house. For others, they traced the community's trust in them to a

Local leadership   69

leadership role that they played in the resistance, which showed they had the 'right' moral character as well as strong leadership experience. For others, it was important that they belonged to the same political party as the national government, with the logic that they would have a better chance of bringing government resources into the *suku*.[11] These explanations often said as much about the *xefe suku* as they did about the community at large; for example, the *xefe suku* of Ainaro explained that he came to be *xefe suku* primarily because he had been the *nurep* in the resistance.[12] Even on close questioning, he did not mention his family's position in the village; it was only when other villagers in the *suku* expressed relief that someone so capable was also from the *liurai's uma lisan*, thus satisfying their customary requirements for legitimate leadership, that this important piece of information emerged.

These, often cross-cutting, factors all point to an important fact: while democratic elections form the *mechanism* through which *suku* leaders are chosen, it is up to the community to elect the person that they judge most able to fill their needs, which include spiritual as well as temporal needs. These complexities are navigated within communities by drawing on the various identities and affiliations that a single individual holds, making it possible for communities to satisfy both customary and liberal democratic notions of legitimate leadership.

While would-be democracy builders interpret the importance of customary authority as potentially dangerous, working against the democratising impact of local elections, what is often overlooked is that the *liurai* is just as tightly bound into this dynamic as the community. Although it has improved over the years, there is still insufficient payment for *xefe suku* to compensate for the effort they must put in, if they are to remain good leaders. A common feature of discussions with such *liurai*/*xefe suku* is the sacrifice that is entailed, with their customary obligations effectively removing their right to choose where they will live, or what work they will do. As the *xefe suku* of Uai Oli explained, his early years were very different to what they are now. Because he was a younger brother he had no customary obligations, so went to live and work in Dili with his family. However, when his older brother, the previous *liurai*, died in 1999, he had to return with his family to his remote community, abandoning his relatively lucrative job, which meant his children were then unable to access the education they would otherwise have received.[13] As he described it, this customary obligation had caused real hardship for him and his family, but he had no choice because if he failed to take on his responsibilities under *lisan*, he would be essentially turning his back on his people.

It is also worth noting that there has always been some flexibility in customary governance arrangements, allowing the recognition of individuals who were perhaps not from the 'right' family. Traditionally, one of the most common methods of doing this has long been through adoption. This was the case with the *suku lia-na'in* in *suku* Fatulia, Venilale, who had been recognised as *lia-na'in* for decades. Even though he was not born into the appropriate family, his capacity was clearly recognised and he was groomed for the position of *lia-na'in*. In order to satisfy customary requirements, his father was adopted into the *liurai* family which put him in the right ancestral line, allowing him to take on the role.[14] In this way, the *suku lia-na'in* could exercise his various competencies without upsetting the ancestors and putting the balance of the community at risk.

As well as customary mechanisms which allowed those who were recognised to take on leadership positions, it also appears that the rights of customary leadership may be taken away – described locally as losing the capacity to talk with *lisan*. As the *suku lia-na'in* of *suku* Fatulia explained:

> For some, our grandfathers and great grandfathers did good things for the people so we get it still because of the justice of *Maromak*.[15] Some, their grandparents did wrong things, lied in order to obtain things so their sons and grandsons don't know how to talk [with *lisan*]. They cannot be *lia-na'in* because they don't know how to talk.[16]

Drawing on this capacity for flexibility in satisfying customary notions of legitimacy, the political dynamic on the *suku* council demonstrates a wide range of methods to satisfy both customary and state-based norms. While state-based governance and *lisan* embody very different ideas of what constitutes legitimate local leadership, local people are negotiating the two systems in ways intended to confer legitimacy through both worldviews. This act of negotiation is eminently practical, seeking to find *xefe suku* who are capable of meeting the various communal needs encompassing both the sacred and the temporal. In practice, the balancing of these multiple identities is what makes it possible for different communities to shape their own governing arrangements in ways that best suit them. Local leaders' capacity to meet both customary and state-based notions of legitimacy also impacts on their effectiveness in carrying out their responsibilities, which, in turn, impacts on the institutionalisation of the *suku* council as a whole.

Gendering of the suku *council*

While it crosses across customary relationships and norms, the *suku* council is clearly a state-based body, and community members consider direct election to be the most important source of legitimacy for *suku* council members (The Asia Foundation 2013, 7). However, as has also been explored, customary ideas of legitimacy for local leadership play an important role in shaping voting patterns, resulting in various hybrid forms of authority that emerge. As a result, some of the norms of customary governance have been translated into the *suku* council's structure and work, resulting in the reproduction of power relationships – and existing inequalities – from customary to state-based governance. While the *suku* council is the acknowledged body representing the community, in practice, the relative effectiveness or otherwise of the council is highly dependent on how well the authority structures of the council reflects the already existing power dynamics within the *suku* more broadly. This is partly because *suku* council members need to work closely with customary authorities in the *suku* – and so need to gain their respect and trust, and work in ways that make sense to them. This dynamic affects different council members in different ways, which goes a long way towards explaining why some are effective within the local sphere and others are not, depending on whether they represent a continuation of previous governing arrangements or are, in fact, a departure from these pre-established customary modes of authority.

The *suku* council is composed of a mixture of 'old' and 'new' institutional figures. The old institutional figures include the *xefe suku*, the *xefe aldeia*, the elder and the *lia-na'in*. The new institutional figures include the women's representatives and the youth representatives. The trust that the 'old' authority figures compared to the 'new' can command in the community is generally pretty high, with the *xefe suku* and the *suku lia-na'in* being especially well-trusted (The Asia Foundation 2013, 9). As was also noted, these institutional figures often must satisfy customary ideas of legitimacy in order to take on the position – *xefe suku* must fulfil the requirements for co-incumbency or authorisation, and the *lia-na'in* must be able to 'speak with *lisan*' on the council, a key reason for him being appointed rather than elected to the council. By contrast, the new institutional figures represent a 'modernising' addition to governance arrangements, and do not need to satisfy customary notions of cultural legitimacy. The capacity (indeed, the *requirement*) of old institutional figures to draw on customary notions of legitimacy goes some way towards explaining the greater level of trust that they are able to command from community members. Because much of their role relies on the community trusting in their lead, this then impacts on their effectiveness in carrying out their leadership responsibilities. And their effectiveness or otherwise in leading the community then snowballs into greater or lesser levels of trust that they are then able to command.

While the combining of customary and state-based legitimacy has assisted the *xefe suku*, *xefe aldeia*, elder and *lia-na'in* in carrying out their roles, it has also resulted in a gendering of the *suku* council, in which the three women occupying reserved seats (two women's representatives, and one female youth representative) have been largely inactive (The Asia Foundation 2013, 14). The general passivity of the women's representatives has been explained in a variety of ways, in particular as a result of the patriarchal attitudes that prevail in the villages, and a general lack of capacity of the women themselves. In their initial report to the United Nation's (UN) Convention on the Elimination of all Forms of Discrimination Against Women (CEDAW) committee, the Timor-Leste government described the predominantly patriarchal foundations of village social structures and *lisan* as the major impediment to women's political participation (RDTL 2009, 61–62). This evaluation was also supported in the Non-Governmental Organisations (NGOs) Working Group's Shadow Report to CEDAW (2009, 9), which further added that the lack of capacity development available for women in Timor-Leste posed a significant problem.

However, while it is clear that there is a problem with the women's representatives, claims of patriarchy and lack of capacity development fail to analyse and place these women's experiences in their local context. In addition, simply offering patriarchy as an explanation for this situation, while true, is also disrespectful to the very real frustration that is experienced by many men who are active on the councils and who would like to see the women's representatives take a similarly active role. Many male leaders assert that they actively look for ways to include the women, rather than deliberately preventing women from doing their work, and there is often a sense of deep frustration stemming from the belief that the women's inactivity causes an unfair addition to their own workloads. As one *xefe aldeia* in *suku* Ainaro bluntly stated, 'Well, I am sorry but there are two women elected, but until now all the work is done by the *xefe aldeia*. We have never received any project from the women's representatives, in all the seven *aldeia* … We, as *xefe aldeia*, when we receive a project, we with the *xefe suku* are the ones in the front line'.[17] This is a common complaint among the *sukus* of rural Timor-Leste, also echoed by the *suku lia-na'in* of Fatulia:

> The *xefe suku* and I as the elder support them. We give them information, and when they don't have a programme we show them, [but] we get mad at them. Because if they have a programme already they have to implement it. 'You don't have a programme, what will you do? As a representative of the women you don't have to answer only to me but to a lot of people – all the people in Fatulia. You don't have the vision to see, to implement your programme' … They need training, training to know about their programmes. Because as they don't have training, if we gave them money they wouldn't do anything and the money would be lost.[18]

The situation is more complicated than most people give it credit for, as it also reflects broader structural issues related to the formation of the *suku* council. Just as blithe explanations of 'patriarchy' are unsatisfying in their explanatory value, simply calling the women 'lazy', as many local leaders do, is equally counter-productive. Important clues can be found if we place these women's experiences in their local context. A Timorese village is a highly stratified social space, and it is extremely difficult for an individual to move outside his or her traditional role, presuming they have a desire to do so. In addition, as well as being a politically difficult space for women to navigate because of rigid notions of gender and class, women carry the additional burdens of caring for their family. Being a *suku* council member is essentially a voluntary position, and council members receive a small monthly stipend to offset expenses. Because of this, only those with a good income stream can afford to take on these roles, which automatically gives it a strong class bias. Women particularly find this difficult as the gendered division of labour often means that women do not have independent income, but they are nonetheless required to keep up their domestic and agricultural labour. As one women's representative explained, while her current position was frustrating in its sense of purposelessness, she wouldn't want to take on the more powerful position of *xefe suku*: 'because the difficulties of the women at home are already a lot, they don't want to go sit in the *suku*, to do the work of the *suku*. This is my opinion, if the people want to choose me for *xefe suku*, I wouldn't want to because there's no money. What would I eat?'[19] Sentiments like these were, and still are, often repeated among village women throughout the country.

However, while patriarchy is real, and it is important to recognise the significance of gender-based stereotypes and constraints, such constraints are not the sole determinants of outcomes. These concerns are also being overcome by many rural women who work as teachers and nurses, community development workers and the leaders of local NGOs, as well as a limited number of women *xefe suku*. They are also being overcome by some women's representatives who have been successful in their roles. It is therefore clear that despite these constraints, these women have been able to carve out a space that allows them to do their work and, to varying degrees, gain the respect of their male colleagues.

In addition, while issues of the gendered access to education might explain the experiences of some women's representatives, it does not provide a blanket explanation. The many different women's representatives I have spoken to over the years cover a broad spectrum of educational and professional experience, ranging from women who are illiterate and only confident in their local language, to highly articulate women who can draw on their leadership experience as bureaucrats and local business owners. Beyond the constraints of social structure and lack of capacity, the inactivity of the women's representatives is also constitutive of broader structural issues directly related to the *suku* council itself, in which it represents a very thin layer of 'modernity' over what are essentially customary relationships. This has resulted in the more conservative gender norms of customary governance being reproduced onto the state institution of the *suku* council, which in some areas has served to both deepen and legitimise those inequalities.

Governance must be for something, and those who govern must fill identified community needs. If they do not, they are unable to maintain their position of leadership within the community and are effectively sidelined. While they may maintain their formal positions of authority until they are voted out of office, their position within the community becomes effectively redundant. It appears that this is what has happened with the women occupying reserved seats on the *suku* councils of Timor-Leste.

When we map authority and leadership roles within a *suku*, it becomes clear that community needs can be filled in two main ways: through resolving community disputes, and through coordinating projects within the *suku*, bringing in new sources of capital for community members. Other work such as collection of statistics for the government and acting as a 'bridge' for external actors to the community is generally for the benefit of those external actors rather than directly responsive to community needs, so is less relevant to their

74 *Local leadership*

local legitimacy. As such, the capacity of individual *suku* council members to resolve disputes and coordinate projects goes a long way to ensuring that they can work effectively and maintain legitimacy with community members between elections.

However, this creates a problem for many women's representatives because dispute resolution via *lisan* is deeply gendered. While disputes resolved via *lisan* ceremonies include a significant number of domestic violence cases, it is often only men who can speak in these ceremonies. This reflects customary practice, where in patrilineal societies, male *lia-na'in* are responsible for resolving disputes and restoring balance to the community. As such, many women's representatives I have spoken to have stated that they are rarely advised and never invited to participate. Unlike the male youth holding a reserved seat who is able to act as the *xefe suku*'s protégé and assist in dispute resolution, the women are unable to take on a role in this important area of community leadership. They are unable to represent women's interests, even in the most serious domestic violence cases. This has had the effect of limiting the institutional and social power base from which they can fulfil their role in representing women's interests within the community. Tellingly, one of the few women's representatives who was happy and comfortable in her position on the *suku* council put much of it down to the *xefe suku*'s support for her participating in customary dispute resolution for domestic violence cases, despite the *suku's* traditions that this should be the preserve of men.[20] The gendered nature of dispute resolution in this *suku* appears to be shifting. But for the majority of *suku* in Timor-Leste, this is not yet the case.

In addition, these dynamics are further cemented by the political economy of local governance, and the current lack of opportunity to implement women's projects within the *suku*. While coordination of women's projects is potentially an important role for the women's representatives to play, it is a consistent complaint across many *suku* councils that while they submit project proposals to the government for funding, they rarely (if ever) receive a reply. This is a reflection of the general lack of state penetration in the villages. Nonetheless, because the women represent recent additions to local governing arrangements, they are unable to call on customary roles and ways of working. As such, the lack of state support appears to have had a much greater impact on the legitimacy of the new compared to the old institutional figures.

In the absence of state support, motivated women's representatives have done what they could, starting various 'women's groups' which drew on existing activities already within the *suku*, such as weaving *tais*, or the planting and harvesting of vegetables. However, because they were not able to bring in new capital or expertise which could substantially improve women's lives, these groups were ultimately unsustainable. The activities – the weaving, the harvesting of vegetables, etc. – did not themselves stop. But the women reverted to their more trustworthy, extended family groups to do this work, in the same way they had done for generations. When it became clear to participants that

Local leadership 75

there was no benefit associated with being in these larger groups because there were no additional resources or other sources of capital, the groups became inactive. As one women's representative in Ainaro explained:

> When we were elected in 2005 we invited the women in the *suku* who didn't have a good [economic] position to work together with us. But because of the poor economic situation our capacity was not enough to do any program ... [The women have] capacity but there is no money so they quit, we could not go forward.[21]

For the few women's representatives who are active in their roles, the capacity to bring new capital or expertise to the women was essential in giving substance to their formal leadership position. Whether they were cooperating with NGO or government breastfeeding programmes, running small women's cooperatives or promoting women's agriculture, to a woman they traced their success to being able to fill identified needs and improve women's lives. Unfortunately for other women's representatives, the introduction of gender quotas without considering how this policy intervention would play out at the local level has set them up for failure, reinforcing existing local stereotypes of the 'uneducated village woman' who lacks leadership capacity.

When analysing the experiences of the women's representatives on the *suku* council, it would be tempting to conclude that women have no real decision-making power in Timorese communities. This conclusion would be erroneous, however, as the interactions between class, gender and age as they fit into state-based and customary spheres are considerably more complex than they might appear on the surface. As has been noted by a number of researchers, there are some women – mostly older women or ex-resistance women – who are strong leaders within their communities (see for example Ospina and de Lima 2006, 51). This was the case with the aforementioned female *xefe suku*, who was elected in part because she came from the *liurai*'s *uma lisan*. There are also many other women who are important in the customary sphere, and who actively exercise their influence. While less common than men, Timor has a long history of women *liurai* and *lia-na'in*. As the head nun of Venilale explained, she often worked with these women rather than the elected women's representatives when she was conducting her health outreach work, because the community listened to them:

> In some villages, the wife of the *liurai* is important. For many of them, the *suku* council is okay but it's not really an authority, just a figurehead – not much else. But some of the older *liurai*, they are always recognised as leaders. So their wives sometimes have more authority. Like in Fatulia, the older *liurai*'s wife is recognised by all the people as a leader. If you need to know something about Fatulia, you can ask her and she can reach the people ... even though she is illiterate ... it is so clear that the people respect her – if she talks they follow.[22]

76 *Local leadership*

While the power of these women should not be over-stated and the overall patriarchal structure of most Timorese *suku* is an important factor that determines the extent of women's influence, it is also clear that there are women who nonetheless command significant authority. Notably also, these women tend to base their authority within the customary sphere, drawing on their influence as a *ferik*,[23] rather than the state-based institutional sphere.

Lessons for institutionalisation

Viewed from the perspective of external stakeholders, the *suku* council is an important (albeit under-recognised) body within Timor-Leste governance, maintaining order within the *suku* and linking the Timor-Leste government to each local community through the provision of statistics and information – for example, by advising the government of who is eligible and requires veterans, widow's or orphan's assistance. However, viewed from the perspective of community members, the *suku* council can be understood as an addition to, and a continuation of, pre-existing power dynamics and relationships. The political hybridity that results as state-based and customary ideas of legitimacy are met holds important implications for how local leadership is gained and maintained.

While the *suku* council is unmistakably a state institution, introduced relatively recently in 2004, it is composed of a mixture of 'old' and 'new' institutional figures, who work within a hybrid local governance environment and who themselves draw on a mixture of state-based and customary ideas of socio-political legitimacy. For the old institutional figures including the *xefe suku*, *xefe aldeia*, elder and *lia-na'in*, this means that they must effectively fulfil both customary and state-based ideas of legitimate local leadership, either through co-incumbency or authorisation models of authority. Their capacity to claim both modes of legitimacy enables them to carry out their role in the community. In addition, and crucially for the Timorese government, the establishment of a council which builds on pre-existing authority figures allows them to claim a presence at the village level without needing to recognise and pay them as public servants.

However, this same set of dynamics also works against the government's capacity to challenge already existing power relationships. While the position of women's representatives is secured by the introduction of reserved seats on the council, these women have been unable to find a substantive role to play in this environment because they are not seen by community members as sufficiently powerful to meet their needs. It is for this reason, as much as lack of capacity or patriarchal attitudes, that women holding reserved seats have been unable to establish themselves as important leaders within the community or on the council. What has resulted is a numbers game, where success in meeting formal targets can be claimed by various agencies in their gender reporting, but little real change to women's leadership is being made on the ground. In fact, the introduction of gender quotas, without any real thought put into the role the women would carry out, may be working against the policy aim by entrenching existing gender stereotypes. This is the risk of bringing policy changes down from 'on high' without taking the challenges of institutionalisation at the local level seriously.

By contrast with putting all our focus on policy 'solutions', if we recognise the fluidity of identity and engagement across state-based and customary spheres of governance, new understandings emerge. The experience of the female *xefe suku* from Soro who was interviewed for this book, or the other women who exercise informal authority in the villages, clearly demonstrates the importance of working with customary authority rather than presuming it is 'in the way' of gender progress. Customary governance should not be placed in a museum; it is lived through the people, and like all forms of governance, it can and does change. Policy interventions that fail to recognise and work with this reality can end up working against their stated aims by reproducing existing inequalities without even realising that this is what they are doing. Nevertheless, recognition of the inherent hybridity and interaction across different spheres may also be transformative, opening up the space for more nuanced interactions, working with local realities and potential points of change – regardless of what 'sphere' they belong to.

Notes

1 Case No. 2/Const/2009/TR.
2 *Tais*: a local, handwoven material which has customary significance.
3 Fieldwork conducted by the author in district Ainaro 2008–2009.
4 Personal interview with *xefe suku*, 23 October 2008, *suku* Ainaro, subdistrict Ainaro (district Ainaro).
5 Personal interview with subdistrict Administrator, 17 December 2008, subdistrict Ainaro (district Ainaro).
6 Personal interview with *xefe suku*, 23 September 2008, *suku* Uai Oli, subdistrict Venilale (district Baucau).
7 Personal interview with *xefe suku*, July 2011, *suku* Uma Uain Kraik, subdistrict Viqueque (district Viqueque).
8 She has since been voted out of office in the 2009 elections.
9 Personal interview with *xefe suku*, 19 December 2008, *suku* Soro, subdistrict Ainaro (district Ainaro).
10 *Rota*: rattan stick, symbolic of the *liurai*'s rule.
11 Personal interview with Susana Barnes, 24 August 2009.
12 Personal interview with *xefe suku*, 23 October 2008, *suku* Ainaro, subdistrict Ainaro (district Ainaro).
13 Personal interview with xefe suku, 23 September 2008, *suku* Uai Oli, subdistrict Venilale (district Baucau).
14 Personal interview with *suku lia-na'in*, 4 August 2008, *suku* Fatulia, subdistrict Venilale (district Baucau).
15 *Maromak*: God. From the traditional perspective, *Maromak* is often interpreted more inclusively than the Catholic definition of God.
16 Personal interview with *suku lia-na'in*, 4 August 2008, *suku* Fatulia, subdistrict Venilale (district Baucau).
17 Personal interview with *xefe aldeia*, 21 December 2008, *suku* Ainaro, subdistrict Ainaro (district Ainaro).

78 *Local leadership*

18 Personal interview with *suku lia-na'in*, 23 August 2008, *suku* Fatulia, subdistrict Venilale (district Baucau).
19 Personal interview with women's representative, 31 September 2008, *suku* Fatulia, subdistrict Venilale (district Baucau).
20 Personal interview with women's representative, May 2012, *suku* Lahomea, subdistrict Maliana (district Baucau).
21 Personal interview with women's representative, 18 December 2008, *suku* Ainaro, subdistrict Ainaro (district Ainaro).
22 Personal interview with parish nun, 8 October 2008, subdistrict Venilale (district Baucau).
23 *Ferik*: female elder.

References

The Asia Foundation 2013. *Reflections on Law 3/2009: Community Leadership and their Election*, The Asia Foundation, Dili.
Boavida dos Santos, A. and da Silva, E. 2012. 'Introduction of a Modern Democratic System and its Impact on Societies in East Timorese Traditional Culture', *Local-Global Journal*, vol. 12, pp. 206–220.
Cummins, D. and Leach, M. 2012. 'Democracy Old and New', *Asian Politics and Policy*, vol. 4, no. 1, pp. 89–104.
Grimshaw, Z. 2009. Interview with Comandante Ular Rihik/Virgilio dos Anjos, conducted October 2009, Dili, Timor-Leste.
Hohe, T. 2004. 'Local Governance After Conflict: Community Empowerment in East Timor', *Journal of Peacebuilding and Development*, vol. 1, pp. 45–56.
NGOs Working Group 2009. *NGOs Alternative Report: Implementation of the Convention on the Elimination of all Forms of Discrimination Against Women (CEDAW) in Timor Leste*, presented to the United Nations CEDAW Committee, New York. Available at: www2.ohchr.org/english/bodies/cedaw/docs/ngos/NGO_alternative_report_TimorLeste_CEDAW44.pdf.
Ospina, S. and de Lima, I. 2006. *Participation of Women in Politics and Decision Making in Timor-Leste: A Recent History*, United Nations Development Fund for Women, Dili.
Ospina, S. and Hohe, T. 2001. *Traditional Power Structures and the Community Empowerment and Local Governance Project: Final Report*, UNTAET and World Bank, Dili.
RDTL 2004. *Decree Law 5/2004 on Community Authorities*, Dili, Timor-Leste.
RDTL 2009a. *Initial Report: The Convention on the Elimination of all Forms of Discrimination Against Women (CEDAW), Timor-Leste*, Government of the Democratic Republic of Timor-Leste. Presented to United Nations CEDAW Committee, New York.
RDTL 2009b. *Parliamentary Law 3/2009 on Community Leadership and their Election*, Dili, Timor Leste.
RDTL Court of Appeal decision, Case No 2/Const/2009/TR, published in the Official Gazette, Series I, No. 28, 5 August 2009.
Tilman, M. 2012. 'Customary Social Order and Authority in the Contemporary East Timorese Village: Persistence and Transformation', *Local-Global Journal*, vol. 12, pp. 192–205.

5 Dispute resolution

All systems of governance have mechanisms in place to deal with disputes when they arise. For most postcolonial nations, this means that there are at least two sets of dispute resolution mechanisms which need to be negotiated within communities: customary processes and state-based law. While negotiating co-existing dispute resolution systems is an important aspect of political hybridity, unfortunately it is also one of the most frequently misunderstood, with analyses quickly degenerating into discussions separating those who are 'for' from those who are 'against' customary systems. This tendency towards polarisation misses the bigger picture.

The tendency to place those who are 'for' and 'against' customary systems into distinct and competing camps is perhaps more pronounced in considerations of dispute resolution because of the normative quality of law, where it is difficult to separate questions of 'what is' from 'what should be'. However, as discussed throughout this book, taking an approach that recognises the reality of political hybridity and the need to engage within this reality requires precisely such a separation.

This needs some explanation. Separating 'what is' from 'what should be' does not mean avoiding the normative question altogether – and it certainly does not mean blithely accepting injustices that are entrenched in the system. All governance systems carry injustices, and it would be inconceivable to suggest – as an academic, an activist and a human being – that we close our eyes to these injustices. But political hybridity is tricky: we are not only grappling with the complexities and contradictions that exist in two distinct governance systems, we are also attempting to understand *how these two systems interact in practice*. If we come into it with a preconceived picture of how things should be, if we come blinded by a lack of self-reflection over our own intellectual baggage regarding what we consider to be 'normal', we miss important pieces of the puzzle.

In the same vein, taking political hybridity seriously cannot be about cherry-picking those aspects that we like, and leaving behind those aspects that we don't. It is more basic than that. History teaches us that customary institutions cannot simply be changed with a stroke of the pen. Nor are they easily replaced with state-based systems. If customary systems were so

80 *Dispute resolution*

vulnerable to outsider intervention, they would have been replaced long ago. Nonetheless change is occurring, led by various pressures which are both internal and external to communities. Change in this context needs to be seen not as something which is *done to* communities, but as one of *active engagement* within communities, as individuals and families seek to make their lives better. This is the governance environment for billions of people around the world. And in order to understand how that change is coming about, we need to understand how communities work.

As previously made clear, for the average Timorese villager, the basic community that they belong to is the web of family relationships which is mediated through their *uma lisan*. Individuals will also belong to many other communities during their lives, including perhaps work communities, political parties, unions or interest groups – but for most Timorese this basic community formed through *uma lisan* is the centre around which other relationships are constructed. As academic Damian Grenfell commonly notes, when Timorese meet each other for the first time their line of questioning is not the common Western class-based preoccupation with what someone 'does'. They want to know where you come from – who your family is, and where the land of your ancestors is.

This mode of social organisation with *uma lisan* at the centre carries two important implications for how disputes are resolved in a village: the first procedural and the second jurisprudential. First, the centrality of *lisan* means that procedurally it is the first point of reference for resolving disputes that arise. There are many different explanations as to why this is so, and the hierarchy placing *lisan* at the centre and state law at the periphery is actively supported by a broad spectrum of local leaders and community members alike.

Second, the need to maintain balance within one's community (and family) forms the basic normative value through which disputes are resolved via *lisan* – bringing us to the jurisprudential side of dispute resolution. Community is the centre for people's continued existence. As such, anything that weakens the community and threatens its continuation needs to be addressed – and balance restored (see for example Trinidade 2008). This has particular implications for issues related to the family unit, such as domestic violence, which was briefly mentioned in the preceding chapter and is examined in more detail later in this one.

Dispute resolution: the procedural elements

Climbing the ladder

The vast majority of Timorese people still prefer to have cases resolved by customary authorities, and only brought into the formal system when local methods have failed (The Asia Foundation 2013, 39). *Lisan* is a localised system which can vary significantly from one place to the next but the basic methods of resolving disputes remain much the same. Across Timor-Leste, when a dispute arises the parties involved will call the *lia-na'in*, the designated

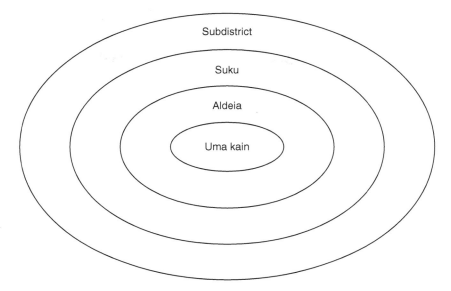

Figure 5.1 Levels of governance in a Timorese village.

customary authority, who will help them to resolve it according to the principles of *lisan*.

Dispute resolution in Timorese villages follows a hierarchy of authority, which is sometimes described as 'climbing the ladder'. This determines how political hybridity is structured in the *suku*, and works as follows. When a dispute arises, the individuals and families involved in the dispute will take it to the local leader who is as close as possible to the disputants. In legal terms this is often referred to as 'the principle of subsidiarity', and in a village it works to ensure that the offence is dealt with quickly and that the leader resolving the dispute is known and trusted by both parties. It also ensures that the *xefe suku* is not overwhelmed with every dispute that arises in his *suku*. There are different leaders in the *suku* who are recognised and empowered to resolve local conflicts. These include a mixture of customary and state-based leaders who occupy the role of either a *xefe* or a *lia-na'in* at different levels of governance. A simple, stylised rendering of the different levels of governance in a Timorese village can be seen in Figure 5.1.

This schema illustrates the hierarchy of leadership as it applies within the village, including those who operate as customary leaders, and those who are either legitimised by election or who exercise delegated authority by elected leaders.[1] Within each level of governance there is generally one *xefe*, but there is often more than one *lia-na'in*. Depending on the governance structure of the village, and guided by their unique *lisan*, these leaders may operate individually or together as a council.

Following this hierarchy, when a dispute first arises, depending on the severity of the offence and how the disputants are related (i.e. whether or not they are within the same *uma kain*, or household), it is taken to the *xefe* and/or *lia-na'in* at the *uma kain* level of governance. If the disputants cannot reach an agreement, it will then be taken to the *xefe* and/or *lia-na'in* at the *aldeia* level of governance, and then to the *xefe suku* and/or *suku lia-na'in*. Sometimes, depending on the unique *lisan* of the community and the needs of the disputants, this process may vary where a council of *xefe uma kain*, *xefe aldeia* and *lia-na'in* may decide on the case, with an accepted hierarchy within that group, before taking it to the *xefe suku* and *suku lia-na'in*. This tends to happen more where an *aldeia* is smaller, and where there is a strong communitarian system still in place.

If an issue is taken to the *xefe suku* and he or she is unable to resolve it, the dispute must then be taken into the sphere of modern law. If it is a civil matter, it may go to the subdistrict administrator for mediation, which often occurs in land disputes. Because of the sensitivity of these issues involving land, *xefe suku* commonly describe their role as *mediating* an agreement between the parties rather than resolving the dispute by making a decision on the outcome. If it is a criminal matter and the *xefe suku* cannot resolve it, the disputants need to take the matter to the subdistrict police. The procedural interaction of customary and state-based systems can thus be understood as a smooth hierarchical process that is mediated by the local leadership, including non-elected customary leaders and the 'old' authority figures on the *suku* council: the *xefe aldeia*, *xefe suku*, *suku lia-na'in* and *suku* elder. Following this basic structure, an unresolved dispute progressively moves 'upwards' from *uma kain* to *aldeia* to *suku* and then ultimately to subdistrict, simultaneously moving ideologically 'outwards' from *lisan* to state-based law.

This structured approach of climbing the ladder is embraced by a broad spectrum of community members and local leaders, for a wide variety of reasons. For those who are perhaps more removed from state-based governance, such as customary authorities, this approach is embraced because it places *lisan* at the centre, respecting its primary importance. As a *lia-na'in* in Ainaro explained, 'Since the beginning we were part of an *uma lisan*, we are from seven *uma lisan*. This is what allows us to follow *lisan*. *Lisan* cannot disappear. As it's said, if our rock is sacred then it is always sacred, if our tree is sacred then it is sacred forever'.[2] The permanence of *lisan* through its connection to the ancestors holds it firmly in place. By contrast, as he went on to explain, the changing nature and seeming arbitrariness of state law, together with the fact that it comes from a long way away (the capital city, Dili), caused him to view it with distrust.

This point on the perceived arbitrariness of state-based law and government was repeated often throughout research undertaken for this book. While an outsider could be forgiven for regarding some of the more remote areas as traditional and disconnected from the politics of Dili, people are nonetheless keenly aware of the distribution of resources and the granting of amnesties that do not benefit them. Corruption, collusion and nepotism are often spoken of as problems in Timor-Leste. The unfairness of payouts to those in the city who had been violent and 'created problems', while people in the villages continue to live in poverty, is expressed often. During 2008 and 2009, the focus was on the resettlement payments that were being made to internally displaced people, or IDPs, who had been affected by the 2006–2007 Crisis. As one *xefe aldeia* of a very poor *aldeia* asked me, 'who is the government helping now? I am sorry but I have to be rude. The people that committed crimes, that destroyed the city, can have a nice house. But the people that stayed calm in this place don't receive help from the government'.[3] To his mind, the injustice of resettlement payouts to internally displaced people who had been responsible for burning others' houses during the Crisis only underlined the arbitrariness of modern power structures and law.

Since the IDPs have been resettled, there has been similar discontent but the focus has shifted to rich government officials who are suspected of stealing from the public purse, the failure to hold to account important people who committed serious crimes during the civil war and Indonesian occupation, and the high level of expenditure in Dili which fails to reach the districts. The topics for discussion may change, but the central thread remains the same. While the phrase 'rule of law' is never used, it is clear that people are very aware of inequalities in how state-based law and politics are playing out, and are drawing their own conclusions as they compare this with how they govern via *lisan*.

Beyond a connection to, and a faith in, *lisan*, there are also more pragmatic reasons for the current reliance on customary authorities in their dispute resolution roles. For example, the *xefe suku* of Fatulia explained that this hierarchy protects him from being overloaded by the number of disputes within the *suku*. For this reason, he actively enforces the hierarchy and will not engage with an issue if it has not first gone through the correct processes within the *aldeia*:

> Sometimes there isn't really a problem but they come to me. And I ask them to tell me what their problem is. Is the *lia-na'in* of your family aware? And I ask them to go back and tell them, and when they cannot solve it they come to me. Then I see if they solved most of the problem. When it is more than my competency I go to the police.[4]

If a case is taken to the police, many local leaders will then maintain it cannot be returned to the *xefe suku* for consideration through *lisan*, as his authority over the matter has not been respected. As the *xefe suku* of Bado Ho'o explained, 'When they go to the police and after that they come to me, then I don't receive them because they didn't recognise me'.[5] Alternatively, if an individual takes the case to the police but then decides to return to the *xefe suku* for resolution, he or she may be required to pay a fine. As was explained by one *xefe suku* of Caicoli:

> When a problem arises in the *suku*, the people must respect local leaders, they are not allowed to take the problem first to the police. If a victim

takes the case directly to the police they embarrass us. So when the problem comes back to the *suku*, they must pay a fine.[6]

From the customary perspective, these rules ensure that people will continue to take the *xefe suku*'s authority seriously. From the modern jurisprudential perspective, this also has the benefit of avoiding 'forum shopping', where disputants could potentially continue to move from one authority to the next until they received an outcome they desired. However, as discussed later in the chapter, it can also have a serious negative impact on more vulnerable members of the community, as they are bounced from one authority to the next and forced to pay a fine if they attempt to access their legal rights.

Walking together, working together

Customary authorities and police in Timor-Leste frequently work together, sharing information and supporting each other. It is not uncommon to find police actively participating in a *tarabandu* or a *nahe biti* ceremony – thereby giving it more weight. In part, this is because individual police are also part of their culture, and have trust in the *lisan* process. In addition, the continuing reality is that the state legal system continues to be critically under-resourced. Given the geographical distances and poor roads, along with the under-resourcing of the police, they tend to rely on disputes being resolved either within the family or within the broader *suku* structure before they are brought to their attention – and so, generally support this mode of dispute resolution.

Reliance on customary authority can extend to quite serious issues. It should not be forgotten that Timor-Leste is a post-conflict nation, and the effects of many decades of war continue to linger in ongoing trauma and violence in the villages. In the year before I went to live in Venilale, many people's houses had been burnt down and people held at machete-point because the members of one political party did not agree with the national election results. However, even a year later nobody had been taken to court, and while the perpetrators of the violence were, and are, well-known to the villagers, it appears unlikely that this would ever happen, partly because the police were also suspected of being involved in the violence. As the parish priest of Venilale explained one evening, 'Here, there are many victims, but no perpetrators'.[7] In an attempt to deal with the ruptures that most recent violence had caused, customary authorities commonly work together with the Church to engage villagers in reconciliation ceremonies, to acknowledge the violence that occurred in the past and to help people to move on.[8]

As well as promoting reconciliation as a way of dealing with past crimes, customary authorities may also be called on to assist immediately when a serious crime takes place. This was the case when a disputed outcome in a 'friendly' soccer match between two *suku* of Venilale led to the brutal murder and dismemberment of one young man from the winning side. Immediately following this crime, violence broke out between the youths which lasted for almost a week, with many injuries resulting from knife-fights and rocks being thrown. During this time, all of the local leaders including the *xefe suku*, *xefe aldeia*, the police, the parish priests and *lia-na'in* – basically, anyone who had authority – worked together in beautifully choreographed cooperation to restore peace, according to their place in the local governance landscape. The murderer was caught by the police and taken into custody, the smaller offences of assault were dealt with first by the police but then were resolved by customary authorities via *lisan*, and the offenders were restored to their communities.

When I spoke to people about how this murder and associated crimes were handled, it was clear that this sharing of responsibility was supported by all of the local leadership. It was practical given the inability of the police – or any other single segment of the local leadership – to deal with all of the issues on their own. It was also necessary to restore peace and promote community cohesion. As the parish priest who was himself from that same village and knew his *suku*'s history explained, while prima facie the murder occurred because a sore loser from a community soccer match was unable to accept the result, there were deeper issues between these two villages, and this murder could be traced as payback for another murder that had occurred many years prior. To deal with the complexity of the case, they needed to employ different strategies. The murderer needed to be removed and the case dealt with through the legal system – by doing this, the space was then opened for pursuing reconciliation. But the focus in resolving the 'smaller' offences of assault via *lisan* was to promote reconciliation by acknowledging this historical context and restoring balance with the ancestors and between different families, with the hope that this would avoid similar murders occurring in the future. To him, given the fragility of the community at this time, this was particularly important. Unlike *lisan*, state law is not seen to hold the same ability to promote reconciliation within a community.

The limits of customary dispute resolution

While respect for tradition is recognised in the Timorese constitution, this does not extend to formally embracing legal pluralism. Recognition of customary authorities only applies in a few discrete areas of the law. However, the reality for the police and others working on behalf of the state is that they are operating in the context of villages that continue to be strongly guided by the requirements of *lisan*. When police are recruited into the force, legal guidelines are not clear on how to work with customary authorities. Nonetheless, they are given sufficient flexibility to ensure that they can work with these authorities – and in general, it is expected that this is what they will do. As such, they need institutional 'links' beyond the hierarchy of authority which satisfies the rules of *lisan*, but is insufficient to satisfy the needs of a liberal democracy. These links have developed as a natural part of the interaction between customary and state-based institutions, and form the basic guidelines for how the police do their work.

One such institutional link that guides which disputes the police should take on, and which are to be left to customary authorities, is that of choice. From the perspective of the police, if the victim of a crime chooses to take a matter to the police then it becomes subject to state-based law. As the chief of police in Venilale explained:

> When these problems happen, when they arrive, the police always ask the victim: what does the victim want? They want to go and solve it in the traditional manner, we prepare a written declaration. We go to *lisan*. If they want to take it forward and they say this is my father, this is my son, the problem happened like this and we want to go forward, then the police make their investigation and take it to court.[9]

At first glance, this institutional link fulfils the principles of a liberal democracy. It emphasises the freedom of the individual to choose, while also being pragmatic in recognising the reality that not everyone wants to take their case to the police. However, if we reflect on the reality of people's lived experience in the villages, there are also political economy issues at play which impact on how this principle works in practice. The lack of resources, the poor roads, and the distances that the police must travel to get to the various communities means that they tend to visit the remote areas perhaps once a month, otherwise relying on the *xefe suku* or other local leaders to advise them of when they are needed. While this is changing, it is still the case that only elite community members tend to own mobile phones. And given the geographical distance of many *suku* from the subdistrict police station, many victims may be unable to make their way there personally. As a result, while there are certainly disputes in which parties may actively choose to have their case resolved via *lisan*, it is impossible to know how many 'silent cases' exist in which, but for these material constraints, victims would prefer to have their case dealt with by the police. As one woman who had suffered through many years of domestic violence explained, 'Some people are educated, some people are rich, but some people are illiterate and really really poor. So I say, we all have rights to take it to court. But I have so many children. I have no money. I don't think the law is really there for me'.[10]

Moreover, the practical reality is that there are many cases in which victims are clearly not given any choice but are simply told by their families and local authority figures to 'choose' customary justice mechanisms, regardless of their own preferences. This is a very common scenario for domestic violence victims. Going to the police is considered synonymous with separation and divorce, and therefore contrary to *lisan*, which focuses on keeping the family together. So a domestic violence victim who looks for help outside customary processes will often be subject to significant pressure to keep it in the family. Sometimes families will pressure a woman to stay out of their own self-interest, and a tendency to blame the victim – as was the case with one woman who was forced to choose *lisan* because the family considered domestic violence a normal part of marriage. As she explained, 'I did not like when they resolved through the family, because this only gave benefit to the family. They could sit together, eat together, and have a party. But there was no benefit to me'.[11] Other times, there may be pressure on the natal family to pay back *barlake* (commonly referred to as 'bride price', in which the groom's family will pay a negotiated amount to the bride's family, in exchange for which the new wife officially enters the husband's family), which they may be unable or unwilling to do. Yet other times, it is more complicated, with the family genuinely believing that if she takes her matter to the police, her husband will leave her with no means of looking after herself and her children. In a subsistence economy context, separation or divorce in a patrilineal system[12] (the majority of Timor-Leste) means that the woman will be cast out of her home and community – with no access to land for cropping vegetables or raising stock. If her natal family is unable or unwilling to take her and her children in, she will have no clear means for survival.

The second commonly-cited institutional link that is used to guide the interaction of customary and state-based law is whether the issue is a 'big' as opposed to a 'small' problem. *Lisan* is generally considered appropriate for 'small problems' such as theft or minor assault, but not considered an appropriate forum for 'big problems' such as murder. As the chief of police in Venilale explained:

> We see to the problem that exists ... A bigger problem that involves death cannot go through *lisan*; then we (the police) have to go. For a small problem, like a problem inside the house, when there is violence between husband and wife, between brothers, between parents and children, this we solve through the traditions we have, but we also work together with the *xefe suku* and other people to solve the problem.[13]

As he went on to explain, there is simply no other way of maintaining community cohesion. While he is hard-working and good at his job, he also explained that the police could not cover every issue on their own with the resources that were available. As such, he said, he was 'always grateful' when a *xefe suku* or other local authority figure resolved an issue before it reached the police.

Across the villages this distinction between 'big' and 'small' offences is generally described as one that is mutually supportive of the principles of both *lisan* and state-based law. From the perspective of customary authorities, the special place of *lisan* as the first port of call is respected. And from the perspective of the police, this process makes sense as it gives them a way to work in the context of limited resources. Finally, it is also seen by both customary and state-based authorities as having the advantage of consistency, where this general distinction is held to apply across all violent acts within the subdistrict. Often, the police will describe this institutional link in terms of the mandate to deal with criminal matters within their jurisdiction, which loosely translates into bigger offences. The smaller offences they describe as civil matters – to be resolved via *lisan*.

Nevertheless, the distinction between small and big problems is often not clear-cut, and closer examination shows that there are many other factors that come into play beyond the severity of the offence. 'Big' offences are indicated by whether there has been blood-letting, however there is considerable interpretative space for other types of injuries, such as bruising, swelling and broken bones. When asked whether such injuries would be taken to the police, the most common answer that is given is 'it depends', and what it depends on varies significantly from one person to the next.

In addition, the principle of taking cases 'where there has been blood' to the police is not always followed. There are still many remote villages with a limited police presence, accustomed to resolving their problems on their own. For these people, it may seem that taking a case to the police is impractical and unrelated to the reality of their lives. While most people know the police and understand their function, a 2013 survey indicates that 49 per cent of the population have not heard of a court and do not understand how it works (The Asia Foundation 2013, 28). And for others, even if they do have a better understanding of the state-based system, it may not make sense to them. As one interviewee explained, 'Many people think that if you just send someone to prison, they eat well and they drink well and they have a house [prison] … There is no change [to the victim's life]. But if they *nahe biti*, the person who did the wrong must pay them for that wrong'.[14] Further, in cases where pursuing reconciliation and restoring balance to the community provides the most important context for dispute resolution, it will likely be dealt with by customary authorities, even if there has been blood-letting. This was the case, for example, with the assaults surrounding the soccer-match murder in Venilale.

And finally, the guiding principle of taking cases where there has been blood-letting to the police is generally not applied to domestic violence cases, which are considered family affairs and therefore in the realm of *lisan*. Even very serious cases of domestic violence may never be taken on by the police. According to people who are working to make the courts and police more accessible to villagers, there are many different reasons which contribute to this tendency, including people not sufficiently valuing the rights of women to be free of violence, economic dependency of women which reduces their ability to access their rights, a lack of responsiveness by the police and courts and concomitant lack of trust in the state-based system – as well as many other interlocking issues. However, one reason often neglected but extremely important is *lisan*'s focus on maintaining balance within the community.

Customary communities are structured through family and marriage relationships formed through the *uma lisan*, and economic relationships are formed and maintained in the same way. Because of this, maintenance of the family unit is of fundamental importance to Timorese customary culture. The inherently conservative focus of *lisan* towards maintaining the family unit in such situations means that when such gendered violence occurs, the *lia-na'in* often attempts to deal with the overall picture by establishing whether in fact the wife has neglected her obligations – or whether the husband has misinterpreted his rights within *lisan*. The role of customary authorities is to protect and ensure the continuation of customary culture – so primary focus in resolving disputes is put on restoring balance in the family, and by extension restoring balance with the community and the ancestors.

In domestic violence situations, this communal focus means making peace between the husband and wife's families, and bringing the family back together. And for many villagers, this communal system works. Their family network provides the fundamental source of their wellbeing, providing them with access to resources, protection and a sense of place. Nonetheless, for women and children who are subjected to domestic violence, this focus on maintenance of the family unit can trap them in a horrific situation with no clear means to escape.

Reproducing inequalities

At this point, it is worth distinguishing between formal processes and the messy reality of dispute resolution in practice. When asking about process, regardless of whether it is written or unwritten, state-based or customary, we are enquiring into a formal set of rules. However, as with any part of the world, the wheels fall off during implementation. Some people are protected more than others. Some types of offences are given more attention than others. The reality of local politics means that the access that different individuals have to customary or state-based institutions varies markedly, depending on other factors which are unrelated to the case, such as the individual's class or gender. Consideration of all of these factors indicates the important point that local processes (both customary and state-based) are not equally available to everyone in the community.

There are many cases in which customary authorities fail to protect women and children from the cycle of domestic violence. However, this does not stop at customary systems. There are also many instances of the police refusing to take on a domestic violence case, even if the woman specifically goes to the police station requesting assistance. This police behaviour was recognised as a serious problem, and in 2010, Law 7/2010, the Law Against Domestic Violence, was passed by the Timorese government, which effectively removed the discretion that had rested with the police and other authorities up until that point. Nevertheless, while this law has changed police behaviour, it has not changed it as much as was hoped. Before the law was in place and the police had greater discretionary powers, it was not uncommon for them to send women back to have the case heard by customary authorities. Since the implementation of the new law, police behaviour appears to have changed, instead replaced with inertia. Instead of sending women back to customary

90 *Dispute resolution*

authorities, it is more common to hear of the police delaying registering the case, asking the woman, who may have children with her, or be nursing injuries, to wait for hours at a time – humiliated – before they attend to her. Alternatively, the police may send her home promising that they will come to take a statement, but never do. This reticence, together with lengthy court delays which may mean the woman waits for years in a shelter before her case can be heard, is creating a chronic distrust in the legal system (see The Asia Foundation 2012). These women are caught in a catch-22, without access to justice in either the state-based or customary system. As one woman explained, for her it was never a case of 'choosing' between customary or state-based systems. For her, it was a question of who has power, and who doesn't. Customary and state-based systems have let her down equally:

> We in Timor, we have law. While we cannot lose our culture, it must always be strong – our culture must walk together with the law. But I see the reality, it is not like that. There is no justice for women. It is only there for people who have money ... The people in Dili need to see that the law is not being applied. Now, women are suffering; men have all the power. They can sleep with whoever they want, get a new wife if they want. But because they give children to us, this makes it really hard for women. I think a lot about this. If I had only one or two children, I could take them to my family. But so many children, my family cannot look after them all.[15]

Research conducted in 2003 on the application of customary law in domestic violence cases identified that an important factor in gaining access and some measure of justice through *lisan* is the capacity and willingness of the victim's family to stand up for her rights (Swaine 2003). Here, too, gender and class intersect. For those women who are more vulnerable, whose family members for various reasons are unable or unwilling to advocate for their interests, local leaders may refuse to hear her case. There are many variations of this. It could be that her family members are all dead, as was the case with one woman I met.[16] It may be because of a 'bad' history, such as another woman who during Indonesian occupation was forced to marry an Indonesian soldier – and since then had been stigmatised as a 'slut' and abandoned by her family and community.[17] Alternatively, it might be because the woman comes from a different cultural group and so is not sufficiently protected by the customary authorities of her husband's clan.[18] Regardless, the outcome is much the same, as existing inequalities and vulnerabilities continue to be reproduced.

This tendency to protect those who are sufficiently empowered, but to sacrifice the interests of those who are not, does not apply to domestic violence cases only. There are many cases in which the rights of those who are more vulnerable – men, women and children – are not sufficiently protected because they do not have sufficient clout in the community. They have no money, or do not have the right connections, or do not have sufficient authority to ensure their rights are met. These and other such cases demonstrate the need to analytically separate the formal rules of governance (whether written or unwritten) from the practical reality of how these systems are implemented. It also speaks to the need to clearly identify where the problems lie, instead of blithely blaming customary systems and presuming that the only need is to become 'more modern'.

'Violensia sivil': modern jurisprudential issues

Close examination of dispute resolution at the local level in Timor-Leste clearly illustrates that customary and state-based justice systems are not simply two parallel legal structures covering the same disputes in different ways. *Lisan* and state law are each driven by different worldviews. In both process and outcome they embody different ways of understanding the relationship between law, community and individuals' rights and responsibilities. Local leaders bring the systems together procedurally through various mechanisms, however there are nonetheless very real tensions between the different values that are upheld by *lisan* and state-based law. To date, because of the absence of overarching legislative guidelines delineating how *lisan* and state-based law should interact, and limited state investment and influence in the rural areas, the everyday decisions of local leaders tend to guide how these two systems operate together. This means in practice that the rules of co-existence are guided predominantly by the requirements of *lisan*. This in turn carries clear implications for the Timorese government's responsibility to protect and promote the human rights of its citizens.

In addition to procedural issues of access to justice, the interaction of customary and state-based law also carries jurisprudential implications. As described previously, it is generally agreed that the police will only intervene in 'big' offences – which they describe as criminal offences. The 'small' offences, described as civil matters, they leave to customary authorities. However, as was also discussed in the previous section, because the preservation of family is at the centre of customary community, there is intense pressure for domestic violence cases to be resolved via *lisan* – regardless of the severity of the offence.

In an attempt to explain why domestic violence is the preserve of *lisan*, sometimes local authorities will speak of a third category of offence specifically for domestic violence cases, referred to either as 'violensia sivil',[19] or violence that is 'perdata'.[20] As one *xefe aldeia* explained, 'regarding violence, criminal violence, we cannot adjudicate. That goes to the police. [But] if it is domestic violence, violence which is *perdata*, we resolve that within the *aldeia*, via *lisan*'.[21] This third category is considered to be in addition to offences which are clearly crimes, and offences which are small, non-violent, and therefore civil – and naturally leads to domestic violence cases being resolved via *lisan*, regardless of whether or not there has been blood-letting.

While this is a neat trick, ensuring that domestic violence cases will remain in the realm of *lisan*, it also indicates deeper jurisprudential issues. Law is written by lawyers, who take for granted the underlying philosophy and jurisprudence which is what links the law to the intent *behind* the law. Nevertheless, when implemented in a context of political hybridity, the jurisprudence can get lost. In this case, the need to negotiate between customary and state-based systems appears to have flipped modern jurisprudential understandings on their head, where in effect offences are considered criminal *because* they are taken to the police, or civil *because* they are resolved via *lisan*, as opposed to the principles of state law where an act is considered criminal based on the seriousness of the offence and the intent of the perpetrator. Through these means, a jurisprudential 'loop' has been created in which most domestic violence cases are defined as civil and therefore resolved via *lisan* – reinforced by a general understanding that they cannot be considered criminal *because* they are resolved via *lisan*.

This jurisprudential loop poses a clear point of tension between customary and state-based institutional spheres. While customary authorities may describe domestic violence as 'civil violence', this does not match the formal description given by the police where, for example, the chief of the police flatly stated that civil violence does not exist – if it is violent, then it is a crime.[22] This is despite the fact that he and I both knew of a number of recent domestic violence cases, resulting in serious injury, which had been resolved via *lisan*.

This tension, and the circumstances in which customary authority has created a third category of 'civil violence', illustrates why we need to understand how people make sense of their local governance environment. Beyond the arcane interest of academics and anthropologists, these dynamics are important because they have real, material consequences in people's lives. While the lack of appreciation for the seriousness of domestic violence tends to be put down to the patriarchal attitudes embedded in customary law (which is no doubt correct) this only tells one side of the story. The other side must also be told: that as a result of the lack of legislative guidelines, the under-resourced police force and the general lack of state 'presence' within the rural villages, the co-existence of the two systems is heavily influenced by the requirements of *lisan* – which is there to preserve the family unit. How these two systems are negotiated in practice is a constant balancing act, which is presently conducted almost entirely by local leaders. The fact that it is a balancing act means that the overall balance can change, although not necessarily in the manner policy-makers tend to presume. Instead of focusing on how to 'get past' the importance of *lisan*, a more nuanced approach might be to work with local leaders, and draw on their legitimacy with the community to develop new, culturally-appropriate preventative and protective mechanisms for women and children victims.

Lessons in hybridity

The hierarchy of dispute resolution that is followed in Timorese villages indicates the centrality of customary governance in a community, in which *lisan* is respected as the first port of call for most disputes. In this context, local leaders have a key role to play in their community, and very often the local police will support them in carrying out this work. There is a range of reasons why this state of affairs continues to be the case in Timorese communities, including the legitimacy that customary processes command with most villagers, and the current inability of state justice institutions to deal effectively with the different disputes that arise.

For many people, this system works. While many villagers have not even heard of important state institutions, such as a court, they are accustomed to their local leaders performing this important dispute resolution role. Local leaders live with them in the same community, so it is expected that they will have a better understanding of their lives, and be able make decisions in accordance with villagers' worldview and values. Placing customary dispute resolution at the centre, and state institutions at the periphery, means that balance with the community and the ancestors is preserved. The place of *lisan* is respected, and customary community, which is vital to a person's wellbeing in a subsistence economy, is protected.

However, for those who are more vulnerable, their interests may be sacrificed to maintain this order and balance. This is the case for many domestic violence victims, and it is common for activists and law-makers to blame the patriarchal nature of *lisan* when they call for reform in this important area of the law. Nonetheless, as has been shown, analyses that focus only on the conservative elements of *lisan* are incomplete, carrying with them the danger that legal reform will be equally incomplete. The reality is that in Timorese communities, customary and state-based 'spheres' of governance do not work separately. They are inextricably intertwined, working in tandem, and inequalities that are entrenched in one sphere tend to be translated into inequalities in the other sphere, as state-based and customary leaders work together to determine the justice options that are available to an individual. Cases in which the rights and freedoms of victims are not respected are not simply due to patriarchal attitudes which are expressed in the continuing importance of *lisan*. Indeed, there is a strong argument to be made for the protective force of family structures and *lisan* in the absence of strong state structures. Those who are rendered invisible and powerless within the local governance environment, such as many domestic violence victims, are often equally let down by the lack of resources, capacities and political will of local leadership within both customary and state-based law.

As these local politics are played out, these more vulnerable members of society are subject to the hegemonic forces that are outside his or her control, as poverty, class, social and family obligations and *lisan* conspire with the state's legal system to leave them disempowered. And in this context, a person's economic capacity is particularly important in determining what justice options are available to them. These realities raise important lessons for the Timorese government – and those supporting them – on how they can engage within a politically hybrid system. It is clearly not sufficient to simply write new laws and policies which enumerate people's rights – or to offer an alternative to customary processes, if people have not heard of state justice institutions and do not trust them. Going forward, it is likely that the current balance that is found between customary and state-based justice resolution will shift over time if state institutions are strengthened. But the importance of maintaining balance with the community and the ancestors means that it is equally likely that customary dispute resolution will not simply disappear – and nor, indeed, should it. This reality places an obligation on the Timorese government to focus not only on strengthening state institutions, but to also consider creative options in which customary institutions can be actively engaged, for example working with local leaders to improve local prevention mechanisms, and other, targeted livelihood assistance for those who are more vulnerable.

Notes

1 As discussed in Chapter 4 of this book, it is also worth remembering that referring to individuals themselves as being either 'customary' or 'state-based' leaders is misleading. It is common for any one individual to source his or her legitimacy through a mixture of customary and state-based means. However, in order to avoid cumbersome descriptions of 'this-leader-who-exercises-legitimacy-through-customary/state-based-means', I will resort to the shorthand of 'customary' or 'state-based' leader to refer to their primary role in the community.
2 Personal interview with *lia-na'in*, 12 December 2008, *suku* Ainaro, subdistrict Ainaro (district Ainaro).
3 Personal interview with *xefe aldiea*, 6 December 2008, *suku* Ainaro, subdistrict Ainaro (district Ainaro).
4 Personal interview with *xefe suku*, 13 September 2008, *suku* Fatulia, subdistrict Venilale (district Baucau).
5 Personal interview with *xefe suku*, 10 October 2008, *suku* Bado Ho'o, subdistrict Venilale (district Baucau).
6 Personal interview with domestic violence victim, June 2012, conducted through a consultancy with The Asia Foundation. Published in Asia Foundation (2012, 7).
7 Personal interview with parish priest, 8 July 2008, subdistrict Venilale (district Baucau).
8 This will always have its limits so long as past crimes go officially unrecognised (and victims uncompensated) by national and international leaders.
9 Personal interview with chief of police, 2 September 2008, subdistrict Venilale (district Baucau).
10 Personal interview with domestic violence victim, March 2012, conducted through a consultancy with The Asia Foundation. Published in Asia Foundation (2012, 13).
11 Personal interview with domestic violence victim, May 2012, conducted through a consultancy with The Asia Foundation. Published in Asia Foundation (2012, 13).
12 Patrilineal: where the woman marries into the man's family. Matrilineal: where the man marries into the woman's family.
13 Personal interview with chief of police, 2 September 2008, subdistrict Venilale (district Baucau).
14 Personal interview with community member, 15 August 2008, *suku* Fatulia, subdistrict Venilale (district Baucau).

15 Personal interview with domestic violence victim, March 2012, conducted through a consultancy with The Asia Foundation. Published in Asia Foundation (2012, 6).
16 Personal interview with domestic violence victim, March 2012, conducted through a consultancy with The Asia Foundation. Published in Asia Foundation (2012, 13).
17 Personal interview with domestic violence victim, April 2012, conducted through a consultancy with The Asia Foundation. Published in Asia Foundation (2012, 13).
18 Personal interview with domestic violence victim, June 2012, conducted through a consultancy with The Asia Foundation. Published in Asia Foundation (2012, 13).
19 *Violensia sivil*: Tetun for civil violence.
20 *Perdata*: Bahasa Indonesia for civil law.
21 Personal interview with *xefe aldeia*, 10 January 2009, *suku* Ainaro, subdistrict Ainaro (district Ainaro).
22 Personal interview with chief of police, 2 September 2008, subdistrict Venilale (district Baucau).

References

The Asia Foundation 2012. *'Ami Sei Vitima Beibeik': Looking to the Needs of Domestic Violence Victims*, The Asia Foundation, Dili.

The Asia Foundation 2013. *Law and Justice Survey*, The Asia Foundation, Dili.

RDTL 2010. *Law 7/2010, The Law Against Domestic Violence*, Dili, Timor-Leste.

Swaine, A. 2003. *Traditional Justice and Gender Based Violence*, International Rescue Committee, Dili.

Trinidade, J. 2008. 'An Ideal State for East Timor: Reconciling the Conflicting Paradigms'. In Mearns, D. and Farram, S. (Eds) *Democratic Governance in Timor Leste: Reconciling the Local and the National*, Charles Darwin University Press, Darwin, pp. 160–188.

6 Economic relationships

The structure of a Timorese village

Community development practitioners have always understood that if an initiative is to have traction, it needs to come from the community and fit into their reality. As a result, community development workers will generally spend a long time coming to understand the community before they attempt to bring in something new – and that 'something new' will tend to be based on assets and strengths which already exist. By contrast, development initiatives which have been introduced from 'outside' the community – whether through the government, international non-governmental organisations (NGOs), donor agencies, or others – tend to come from a different paradigm, which puts their own structures first and therefore fails to fit into local realities and institutional structures. This can result in many missed opportunities. Worse than missed opportunities, it can also create new problems, as it may deepen existing fracture lines in the community, reproducing and exacerbating existing inequalities in the village. While these dynamics tend to be invisible to 'outsiders', they are nonetheless extremely important to the villagers who must live with the results of their interventions.

Understanding the impact of these development interventions requires a basic understanding of village political economy. As discussed already, in the villages of Timor-Leste there are recognisable patterns through which state-based and customary institutions are engaged to fill communal needs. These patterns structure engagement between elected *suku* council members and customary authority figures within the *suku*, who work together to meet complex communal problems in the context of limited resources. This in turn shapes how disputes are settled, resources distributed and projects coordinated in the context of co-existing state-based and customary governance institutions. Through these dynamics, political hybridity is given shape so that it forms an overall system of governance which people understand and can engage in.

In most cases, family networks form the first layer of governance that individuals encounter, and this is where community governance begins, moving through the three important 'layers' of customary community: the *uma kain*, the *aldeia* and to a lesser extent the *suku*. These communities have been central to local Timorese governance since pre-colonial days, so customary institutional structures define, in a very real sense, membership of the communities themselves. This in turn carries important implications for economic and political life. As well as holding spiritual and ethical significance, *lisan* and the familial networks through which it has developed and is maintained, also holds political and economic significance as it structures communal relations. Through these familial networks, hierarchies of leadership are maintained, disputes are settled, access to land and resources is governed and economic dependencies are maintained.

The importance of *lisan*, and *uma lisan*, is not simply because of their spiritual significance, although that is certainly fundamental. As Damian Grenfell *et al.* (2008, 13) demonstrate, *lisan*, with its emphasis on maintaining and balancing the community, is foundational because it has kept the community together despite war, famine and other massive social upheavals. At the *aldeia* level, *lisan* is actually constitutive of the community itself: as *aldeia* are not officially mapped, the same familial structures that underpin *lisan* often define, in a very real sense, membership of the *aldeia* itself. This translates into complex local authority structures, as the authority structures which are maintained through the customary system are naturally entwined with how the community identifies itself.

This understanding of community as based on family rather than territorial boundaries, while conforming to local understandings of identity, does not always lend itself to administrative convenience. For example, across Timor-Leste there are some 'split' *suku*, where, rather than being a single territorial unit, a *suku* is spread across two distinct territories, separated from each other by another *suku*. The split nature of these *suku* and the difficulty in looking after the needs of the people who live in the faraway regions make governance a difficult proposition for the *xefe suku*, particularly during the wet season. However, as the *xefe suku* of one such *suku* (Bado Ho'o) explained, there are important historical reasons for this split territory, which cannot be easily addressed:

> Our *suku* is the original kingdom. It came like this, it was not in our time that we chose each other ... I don't know if in the future there are going to be changes, how they are going to make the borders between *suku*. This would need more profound research from this government, for things to go well. But this came from a long time ago – you can see for yourself, the people are far from each other, they are never close. Other people can be close to me but people from my *suku* can go live far in [the *aldeia*] Uai Cana, some go to Badu Mori, some are close in Bercoli ... To change this it has to be from the government, through laws, because our origin is like this – in our tradition we don't separate from each other even if we live far away from each other.[1]

As the *xefe suku* went on, this division of territory made it difficult for him to ensure that everyone had access to services, and that things are run fairly and

98 *Economic relationships*

well. While he tried to visit the villages disconnected from the main territory in which he resides, it was difficult to do this regularly. The constraints posed by this division of territory meant, in practice, that he was heavily reliant on the *xefe aldeia* in the far-off villages to keep order, manage conflict, and link the population with different service providers if necessary.

While split *suku* are a very obvious example of community formed through customary relationships and family connections, similar dynamics also apply in other *suku*. Another very interesting example can be seen in *suku* that are close to the border with Indonesia. For these communities, the borders between Timor-Leste and Indonesia are often very fluid, and customary relationships between villages on either side of the border are strong. This can have both positive and negative impacts. On the negative side, the border between Timor-Leste and Indonesia is frequently compromised as people engage in their daily lives, and opportunists take advantage of this fluidity to illegally smuggle people and goods across the border. On the positive side, customary relationships can also be capitalised on to address cross-border conflict. This can be seen in the enclave of Oecusse, where there are regular problems with ex-militia now residing in Indonesia, who enter Timor-Leste to murder villagers and burn their houses (Fundasaun Mahein 2012). As the government of Timor-Leste has had little traction in dealing with the Indonesian government over these issues, and border patrols are too weak to properly protect the citizens, village leaders have worked together with relevant government ministries to hold a major *tarabandu* ceremony, prohibiting these ex-militia from engaging in such violence.[2] It may not stop the violence altogether, but such measures can nonetheless work to minimise it, increasing communities' capacity to address their own needs rather than being wholly reliant on the two governments adequately securing the border.

Perhaps because of the focus on family as the central unit for customary governance, much important governing tends to be carried out at the *aldeia* and *uma kain* levels. This is reinforced by the practical reality of providing for villages that, in the rural areas, tend to be small and scattered – reflecting communities' historical origins and connection to the land of their ancestors. The scattered nature of many communities can make service provision extremely difficult. Local leaders commonly speak of the difficulties around the lack of access to schools and health clinics, lack of electricity, lack of water supply, and even difficulty in planning roads because, as one *xefe suku* put it, 'people don't like to live in a straight line',[3] reflecting the very real challenges in catering to a diversified population. This dynamic of small, scattered communities has intensified since independence. During Indonesian occupation, people were forced to live in concentrated areas so that the authorities could regulate their movements. However, when independence came, many communities chose to return to their traditional lands (McWilliam 2005).

Given these various factors, it is normal for the *xefe suku* to rely on *xefe aldeia* to do the day-to-day governing and to act as a 'bridge' between him or her and the population. As we saw in the previous chapter, *xefe suku* actively support and enforce this principle of subsidiarity, sending community members back to their *customary leaders* if they come to them with a problem. While this works to ensure that governance is based on customary understandings of community and fits in with the political economy of a Timorese village, it can also result in a disconnect between local governance norms and externally-led development. From the community perspective, customary institutions of governance are equipped to manage economic relationships and associated issues of distributive equity and resource management at the *aldeia* level. Nevertheless, because of economy of scale, most externally-driven 'local' initiatives tend to stop at the subdistrict or *suku* level of governance where customary institutions and understandings of authority are more complicated. This can make these projects difficult for local leaders to manage in a way that community members consider legitimate.

Customary economic relationships

The most common everyday interactions of most people tend to be within and between *uma kain*, where members hold important obligations to each other. Out in the more remote villages, this tendency is even more pronounced. However, unlike dispute resolution – which is highly formalised – these economic relationships tend to be more fluid, maintained through a mixture of formal customary institutions that dictate the hierarchy of leadership, and economic dependencies that flow from this hierarchy of leadership and uneven access to resources.

These economic relationships are closely linked to the importance of subsistence agriculture in Timor-Leste, which is the main source of income for the majority of the rural population. In this context, access to and use of land is of primary importance. Unlike much of Southeast Asia where the landlord-tenant model of land use underpins important power relationships within a village, land tenure in Timor-Leste is highly individuated, with residential land, gardens and plantations held and managed by individual families rather than collectively as part of a larger group (Fitzpatrick *et al.* 2012). This system of land tenure, one that is focused on individual families, means that customary institutions at the level of *uma kain* are of vital importance for people's economic wellbeing. At the centre of village political economy are family relationships. These relationships are maintained through a mixture of formal customary institutions which dictates the hierarchy of authority, decision-making, access to resources and mutual obligation within the broader family structure, and economic dependencies that flow on from that hierarchy and uneven access to resources. Depending on where they fit into the family hierarchy, different family members have varying levels of access to family resources. Family patrons – those at the top of the family hierarchy – have privileged access and rights over important resources, such as land. This is balanced by an expectation of patronage for those family members who are lower down in the hierarchy.

Other central customary institutions that guide economic relationships are those revolving around marriage relationships, in which the two families are brought together through ritual exchange. There are different types of customary relationships, depending on whether the clan is matrilineal or patrilineal. For the majority of Timorese communities, which are patrilineal, customary obligations are shaped through the institution of *barlake*, or 'bride price'. While *barlake* is often simplistically interpreted by outsiders as men 'buying' and then 'owning' their wives, culturally it has much deeper roots. Historically, the institution of *barlake* was a method of bringing two families together and creating between them an ongoing relationship of mutual obligation. In some parts of Timor-Leste, the *folin* (or price) is set extremely high so as to ensure an ongoing 'debt' that one family has to another, which continues to cement this relationship through the years. The importance of customary institutions and exchange through marriage lies in the fact that it brings different groups together in relationships of mutual obligation. These kinship lines are complicated and spread beyond the village, crossing language and clan groups all over Timor-Leste. Customary relationships formed through marriage and underpinned by *barlake* were particularly important during times of war, as one clan could call on another to support them in their battles (Schulte Nordholt 1971, 388).

In contemporary village life, while there is little use for clan war, *barlake* is nonetheless central to *lisan* relationships. However, it is now considered controversial in many Timorese feminist circles, as it is blamed for ongoing inequality between men and women in a family relationship and a contributing factor to gender-based violence – and in some cases, there is truth to this statement. There are certainly cases that have been documented by NGOs, in which the institution was (mis)interpreted by men who wrongly believed they 'owned' their wives and thus had the right to beat them. In one such case, a man in Ainaro argued that just as he had the right to 'break his crockery' if he so desired, he also had the right to 'break his wife'.[4] Nevertheless, customary authorities will also insist that such understandings are a gross misinterpretation of the institution, that *barlake* is about bringing families together – and cannot be understood in such individualistic terms as a man 'owning' his wife.

While *barlake* needs to be understood as a Timorese institution focusing on families rather than individuals, as a customary institution it nonetheless has material impact on people's lives as it shapes relations within the *uma kain*. It is at this broader systemic level that it works, by placing expectations on the woman that her first loyalty must now be to her new family. And when these expectations are not met, problems may occur. For example in one case I became aware of, the husband violently 'disciplined' his wife because she continued to provide food to her natural parents and this was thought improper, as she should now be providing for her new family.[5] But this is quite different to a misunderstanding that the husband 'owns' the wife.

As it is so entrenched in economics, it can also contribute in a roundabout way to violence perpetrated by mothers-in-law against daughters-in-law. In a modern economy, it is not uncommon for unemployed sons to rely on their mothers to provide *barlake* so they can marry. However, 'paying' for her son's wife can create an expectation that the daughter-in-law should 'repay' through taking on extra work in the household – and when the daughter-in-law resists this expectation as unfair, tensions can emerge which may erupt into violence. Young women are particularly vulnerable to older women as they share the workload with other women in the house, but can remain relatively immune from the men of the house who have little say over how the household work is divided. The mother-in-law sees it as only fair that she be repaid, the daughter-in-law sees it as distinctly unfair that she be expected to do both her and her mother-in-law's work in the house – and neither are given the tools to analyse the impact of the gendered division of labour which leads to such tensions.

Despite the gendered impact of *barlake* in such cases, women and men alike will commonly defend the institution, including some highly articulate professional women who, when questioned, simply state that customary institutions are important and need to be respected, but that *barlake* is at times misinterpreted. While many people embrace the idea of the *folin* being reduced to alleviate pressures in the household – allowing people to pay for their children's schooling, or food, or health care – there are few who state they would welcome *barlake* being abolished altogether. These responses indicate the deeply embedded nature of the institution – and the need to tread carefully and avoid assumptions before working to address its negative elements.

In a village context, it is perhaps not surprising that people are so firmly supportive of these institutions. Beyond accounts of 'the simple villager who knows no better', which unfortunately still permeate discussions of customary governance, the undeniable fact is that these institutions provide for people's livelihoods and wellbeing, however imperfectly. In the absence of a broad social security system, family patrons are expected to look after vulnerable family members, and the economic and social needs of widows and their children are supported through the wider family network. 'Family policing' is also common. In Venilale, for example, a husband who had effectively abandoned his family but was employed by the family business in Dili had a portion of his wages regularly deducted to provide income for his wife and children back in the village. These family obligations are reciprocal, as those in receipt of family support have obligations in turn to their family patrons in a complex hierarchical system of exchange – generally, through the provision of labour or food. Such systems of mutual obligation ensure the continuation of the family and the community, as people operate through a shared understanding that they need each other. Customary understandings of how work should be shared varies from one place to the next, but a common division of labour is of women holding responsibility for the upkeep of home and family as well as cropping vegetables, men being responsible for the heavier work in the fields, and children also having significant responsibilities. Family patrons are generally regarded as having responsibility to look after the vulnerable members of their extended family, including widows and their children. And as the institution which binds families together, it is *barlake* which lays the customary basis for these mutual exchanges.

Customary institutions that guide the hierarchy of decision-making and resource distribution create tight economic dependencies that are maintained in these small communities. We have seen that they actively work to shape and recreate gender and marriage relations in a community. The same also applies to class, as the opportunities that are available to people are shaped according to the *uma lisan* they belong to, and according to where they fit into the extended family hierarchy. In a subsistence agricultural society, much employment is maintained within the family unit, as family patrons fulfil their obligations to vulnerable family members by giving them access to land or other resources in exchange for their labour.

However, many of these relationships tend to fall outside the formal requirements of customary institutional structures and are determined more by the economic dependencies that are shaped through and by these institutions. As a result, while family patrons may be beset by constant requests from family members (vulnerable or otherwise) for money and other resources, how they choose to fulfil their responsibilities is ultimately up to them. At one end of the spectrum, I have come across situations where the family patron took out a bank loan in order to meet the constant requests for cash by unemployed family members. Nevertheless, in other families, the patron may pay very little attention to the requests from family members. Across the villages of Timor-Leste, this can result in quite uneven sharing of resources, depending on the relative generosity of family patrons.

In addition, the family 'social security' network is not foolproof. There are situations where the protective unit of the family is, for various reasons, no longer functional, leaving its members especially vulnerable. This was the case with an Ainaro man, whose family had been killed during the occupation, and whose closest relative was a distant nephew. When he was afflicted with a stroke that left him paralysed and bedridden, there were no family members who saw it as their responsibility to care for him and give him food. This man remained alive only because of the outreach work carried out by the Ainaro nuns, who brought him meals every couple of days and who built the small house in which he lives. The nuns had tried the easier option of giving sacks of rice and asking his nephew's wife to cook it, but this did not work as he was unable to defend himself when the neighbours simply took the rice for themselves. Cases such as these illustrate what can happen if the protective force of the family unit is removed.

Contemporary village economies are not just governed by customary institutions. While the subsistence village economy, which is guided by differentiated access to land and expectations of labour, is still central to most people's existence, there are also wider economic influences which impact on people's lives – both positive and negative. For some, avenues for greater economic independence outside customary relationships can have a transformative impact. As one woman who had escaped a domestic violence situation related:

> Now, it is much better. In the past, I had to do everything according to what [my husband] wanted. I had to look after the house, look after the animals, crop the vegetables, sell them at the market. When I went to the market I would sell the vegetables. Then he would ask me to account for all of the money I got. So I would give it all to him. If I needed money, I needed to ask permission from him. But now, no. Now, I can earn my own money, I can look after my own life. I can look after myself and there is no one to tell me that I can't do things, there is no one to stop me from doing things or getting value from my work.[6]

For this woman, the economic opportunities open to her in the wider community made all the difference, allowing her to work towards a better life. However, there are also many challenges as customary relationships and dependencies are becoming increasingly strained and capitalist economic forces becoming more prominent in the villages. For some, the increased mobility can strain women's wellbeing as greater numbers of men move to Dili to escape poverty and women are expected to remain at home, looking after their children. Unless remittances are sent back to their families in the village, this leaves their wives and children in the villages more vulnerable than ever. The unfortunate fact remains that, given unemployment levels in Dili, the more common scenario is of a man who is barely able to meet his own needs, let alone have any extra to send back to the village.

Segmented and potentially fractured

There are two important points to note about customary institutions as they relate to economic structures. The first point is that customary institutions in Timorese communities are essentially 'inward looking'. Perhaps linked to the fact that subsistence agriculture remains the primary source of income, customary institutions have developed to govern the use of resources which already exist in a community. In the main, they have not evolved to govern resources that enter the community from outside – and where such institutions have evolved to manage external resources, they are often not as strong as those governing the use of pre-existing resources such as land.

The second point is that because Timorese communities are small and scattered, the 'natural' units for economic cooperation are equally small and scattered. As a general principle, the strength of customary institutions, including customary land tenure and *barlake* and corresponding economic dependencies, makes the *uma kain* and *aldeia* the 'natural' groupings within a *suku*. Of course, it is also true that the social capital which exists varies significantly from one *aldeia* to the next, and customary affiliations based around *uma lisan* often do not correspond directly to *aldeia* borders. Nonetheless, for the broad purposes of understanding local communities and how they relate to each other both internally and externally, the segmented nature of *suku* is important to understand. Beyond the *uma kain* and *aldeia*, larger *suku* communities tend to only come together at the behest of local leaders.

The smaller communities of *uma kain* and *aldeia* can of course be ruptured, and there are many examples of this happening during the difficult struggle for independence against Indonesian occupation. However, as Andrew McWilliam (2005) relates, this is not the norm. Viewing governance as it is experienced from within a community, *suku* should therefore be understood not as a single cohesive unit that is governed by the *suku* council and headed up by the *xefe suku*, but rather as a collection of *aldeia*, within which are a number of *uma kain*. As a general principle, a *suku* is always segmented and may also be fractured – depending on the history of conflict in the area. This in turn dictates how well the smaller communities that provide the building blocks for larger *suku* communities can work together.

Because of this local specificity, the overall cohesion of the *suku* will therefore vary significantly from one *suku* to the next. This can mean that while one *suku* can be relatively easy to govern, a neighbouring *suku* can be extremely difficult to govern. Such variation is attributable to many factors, including the pre-existing customary structure of the *suku* that is unique from one clan to the next, the impact of colonial history in co-opting indigenous governance structures, the impact of the civil war, Indonesian occupation and the resistance movement, and also the impact of other modern external influences – for example, the opening up of the market economy and affiliation with new groups and political parties. These various factors, together with the influence of local leaders as they operate within this governance environment to pursue their political agendas, has a direct flow-on effect as to whether a *suku* can be considered segmented but nonetheless reasonably cohesive – or internally fractured. All of these factors have a direct impact on how well the community can work together to implement projects or pursue other opportunities to develop their *suku*.

Project management in a segmented suku

Across the villages of Timor-Leste, there is a pressing need for essential infrastructure, including new school buildings, health clinics, housing (especially where homes were destroyed in the violence of 1999 or 2006/2007), access to electricity and water, and sanitation. More broadly, irrigation channels need to be built, roads and bridges need to be built or rebuilt, and basic agricultural machinery is needed to assist with food security. There are equally pressing needs for social or human investment, such as teachers, doctors, nurses and midwives to fill the schools and health clinics, assistance in developing small businesses, assistance for vulnerable members of society, and the very difficult 'community building' or 'reconciliation' work required for communities still traumatised by recent violence. This is the typical picture of most of the 442 *suku* across Timor-Leste, and almost every *xefe suku* I have spoken to has expressed frustration at their inability to provide for their community. As a result, the more active *xefe suku* will work very hard to attract external assistance from different actors – the government, NGOs, and, if they have a small grants scheme, donor agencies.

However, while these investments are particularly important in addressing the feeling of disenfranchisement of rural communities from the Timorese state, careful examination of community dynamics also demonstrates that this inflow of resources has prompted internal conflict that existing institutions cannot always contain. Partly, this is because of a lack of understanding of external stakeholders around the competition for resources which is spurred on by poverty. For poorer community members, even small investments can make a real difference, and if they are unable to share in the benefits, social jealousy and allegations of corruption inevitably arise. Partly, as well, it is because of a mismatch between internal and external definitions of what 'working locally' means. For external actors, economies of scale dictate that even very small development projects tend to be too large to coordinate with *aldeia* communities – the 'natural' grouping in a *suku*. When implementing locally, NGOs and government therefore tend to focus on the *suku* or subdistrict level of governance. This then means that they will often rely heavily on the *suku* council, and the *xefe suku* in particular, to provide guidance and to make important decisions as the project is being implemented. While the *xefe suku* theoretically operates as part of a council, the reality is that as head of the council, the *xefe suku* holds most power. In practice, therefore, the choice lies with the *xefe suku* as to how much he or she chooses to involve the other members of the council or other members of the community when implementing particular projects. This then opens the door to various forms of nepotism. As one community member explained:

> Sometimes *xefe suku* give us help to do some work or some programme. They don't use the democratic system, they use the individual system. This is just an example: today I work, in the future I will work again because he knows me. I am the only one who works. But he doesn't look after a lot of people ... A lot of people are smart but he doesn't need them.[7]

Similar sentiments were expressed by a *lia-na'in* from the same *suku*: 'when [a project] involves money or jobs they look after their family first. The *xefe suku* is my family. I am old but I can see when things aren't right. When there is some work he only gives it to his family and friends'.[8] Such situations are common. Even for *xefe suku* who are known to be actively engaged with their community, community members will often note that even if he is providing much-needed infrastructure for the benefit of all, the important issues around who are employed as labourers to, for example, build a school, are decided personally by the *xefe suku* – which means in practice that his community, and his family, are the first to benefit. Such dynamics can result in serious issues within a community, deepening underlying fracture lines as the project benefits some and not others.

These fracture lines can be very deep. For example, in the *suku* of Cassa in subdistrict Ainaro, there is a deep rift that formed during the Indonesian occupation between families who were pro-autonomy, and others who were pro-independence. When in 1999 the people voted for independence, the pro-autonomy militias were exceptionally brutal and many people were killed or taken as hostages to West Timor, and this rift is now expressed in ongoing conflict between the larger family groups. The deep divisions caused by these actions are now being translated into land disputes where, depending on who is describing the dispute, pro-independence families have either claimed or reclaimed their land from pro-autonomy families. As the *xefe suku* explains, these are intractable disputes: 'it is a little bit difficult because this is a political issue ... Regarding *lisan*, they will not sit together. They only come to us for us to listen to them, but they don't listen to the subdistrict administrator or the district administrator'.[9] However, the elders in this *suku* also make the point that the conflict did not begin during Indonesian occupation. As they relate the history of the area, many of these conflicts between different family groups have been going on for many generations, reflective in part of different ethnic origins of different groups.

There are similar issues being played out across Timor-Leste, where there are complicated disputes with competing claims through Portuguese, Indonesian and customary land tenure systems. There are also many issues where the displacement of people escaping violence and vacating their property meant that others came in and took possession, or where land title granted during Indonesian occupation is now being contested. These disputes can be extremely divisive, deepening already existing fracture lines within a *suku*.

These divisions in a community are further inflamed if there is no sharing of financial details of how resources are being distributed, which is a common enough occurrence. As one *xefe aldeia* explained:

> Sometimes the district administration gives to the *suku* and the *xefe suku* is in charge of it. How they distribute it to the *aldeias* and how much money there is, we don't know. When they come to the *aldeia* they ask us to work. But ... they don't tell us how much money came from there, how much are they distributing to us. They never tell us how much it is, they only ask the people to work. I know that there is a lot of money, but until now they haven't told us.[10]

This was clearly a point of deep frustration for him: when pressed for details, how one would go about getting this financial information if they wanted it, he was uncharacteristically blunt, replying that he didn't know, that he had

Economic relationships 107

never seen any financial documents, but that the paperwork 'is probably at the *xefe suku*'s house'.

It all comes back to perspective. On the one hand, while projects may appear to be well-implemented from the external perspective – as is likely with programmes that have checks and balances built into them to ensure that resources are properly expended – the picture from within a *suku* may look quite different as issues of distributive equity arise, fanning underlying conflicts within a *suku*. In addition, the lack of transparency within the *suku* council, and the tendency of the *xefe suku* to work alone or with people of his choosing, has a direct impact on the democratising potential of *suku* council, undermining the community's ability to hold their elected representatives to account. While community members may attempt to gain financial or other information about these projects, they are frequently stymied in their efforts and it is often unclear even who has the relevant documents – whether they are with the *xefe suku*, the implementing agency (government or NGO), or someone else entirely.

On the other hand, the lack of trust and resultant conflict does not always indicate that there is corruption or even nepotism as it is commonly understood: it is also simply indicative of the structure of the *suku*. In coordinating an incoming project for the *suku*, the *xefe suku* must work through the *xefe aldeia* who in turn will coordinate with *xefe uma kain* to smooth the way for the project and provide labour if necessary. Except within his or her own *uma kain*, this coordination is generally something the *xefe suku* is unable to do alone, as he or she often does not hold sufficient social power with other *uma kain*. Nevertheless, the *xefe suku* wields economic power, and is responsible for deciding how to allocate external resources in the *suku*. Reflective of this division of power, and in the context of very poor villages, the relationship between *xefe suku* and different *xefe aldeias* can be tense as different individuals manoeuvre for a more favourable division of resources. As one *xefe suku* explained:

> The *xefe aldeia* is elected by the people but some of them only follow their private interests ... Some bring issues from the people to us; some never bring the interests of the people to us. They kind of close the way to the people ... We as *xefe suku* always make them do programmes for the people, but when we don't follow what they want, they [*xefe aldeia*] can close the way and we cannot do anything.[11]

For this *xefe suku*, the only way to avoid the frequent allegations of corruption that were levelled by *xefe aldeia*, and the generally high levels of distrust and contentious nature of local politics in this *suku*, was to evenly apportion NGO income to each *aldeia* for them to implement smaller projects. However, while this strategy has been successful in protecting the *xefe suku* from allegations of corruption and incompetence, it has been less successful for the projects themselves. As he went on to explain, the money had at times been wasted in unsustainable investments such as buying machinery that the community then did not have the capacity to maintain, and limiting efforts to engage in broader, long-term planning. And the results were often not in the best interests of the *suku* as a whole as they didn't take into account the needs of the broader *suku*, and could not take into account economies of scale. Nonetheless, this strategy achieved its role in protecting the *xefe suku* from what was otherwise an unmanageable set of local politics.

From the 'outside', it is easy to label a *xefe suku*'s preference for giving benefit to his family and community as nepotistic or even corrupt. However, when viewed from inside a community it becomes clear that there is a combination of social forces that might lead a *xefe suku* down this path. From the perspective of the *xefe suku*, giving much-needed work to his or her own family members may reflect the fact that he or she is attempting to fulfil customary obligations and also get the work done in time and up to standard in the context of a fractured *suku*. He is not alone in taking this approach. Other community members, if they also have the power to distribute resources or work, do the same thing. The reality is that he is better able to effectively lead members of his own community who, because of customary relationships, accept his leadership as legitimate. He is also in a better position to sanction those who under-perform. Those who come from a different community, by contrast, feel no such customary obligation – and may in fact be antagonistic to the leadership that he exercises.

It is therefore not surprising that many interventions that are more externally-driven have not had the same success in communities. There is a clear connection between the relative success or failure of different government programmes, and the capacity of programme implementers to involve communities in the planning and implementation of different projects. Over the past five years, the government of Timor-Leste has implemented a range of different rural development programmes – including the *Pakote Referendum*, the *Programa Dezenvolvimentu Lokál (PDL)*, the *Programa Dezenvolvimentu Desentrilizadu (PDD)*, the *Planu Dezenvolvimentu Integradu Distrital (PDID)* and the *Programa Nasionál Dezenvolvimentu Suku (PNDS)* – all of which are intended to increase infrastructural development in the rural areas and to encourage local economies. These various programmes have all varied in their specifics, but a broad comparison of their relative success or failure indicates two themes which are important: the programme's inclusion of communities at all stages of the project cycle, and the integration of the programme with other government initiatives that also operate in the community, both of which are central to a successful project (The Asia Foundation 2012a).

For these various programmes, a key point of project and programme failure has revolved around the extent of community involvement in project selection and planning, implementation, and operations and maintenance. In some instances, the failure of engineers to draw on local knowledge of water flow during the wet season has resulted in roads that were washed away during the rainy season, or tanks that are rendered unusable. In other instances, while projects were up to technical standard, they were located in illogical places making them essentially unusable. For yet others, projects were halted halfway through because of opposition from customary authorities or others over the use of land or other resources (The Asia Foundation 2012a, 31–32).

There are many potential issues that can arise – depending on the reality of local politics in an individual *suku*. During my time spent in many different villages across Timor-Leste, I have encountered numerous failed projects and community conflict that is born through seemingly 'small' issues, which are nonetheless of fundamental importance within a village. The social dynamics that result in 'winners' and 'losers' in a *suku* can be analysed both in terms of process and outcome, which play out in different ways across a project's life-cycle. Sometimes, only a few individuals are involved in the decision of what projects should be implemented. Other times, there are issues over the use of land or other resources, as roads are opened up without realising they run directly through sacred sites, or the family whose land is used then take the opportunity to charge fees for the use of what should be common infrastructure. Very often, the infrastructure is not adequately maintained, as there is no clear agreement around who in the community will be responsible for operations and maintenance, and community members unsurprisingly state that the external party – whether government or NGO – should be responsible for the cost of maintaining it, as it was their idea to build it in the first place.

All of these issues pose very real problems for communities, and also for government officials who are responsible for implementing the programme. For district and subdistrict officials, the incapacity of top-down programmes to allow them to take these issues into account is a key source of frustration, directly impacting on their capacity to manage potential sources of conflict, and diminishing the trust that community members have in them and the rest of the government. As the district administrator of Baucau described:

> Some projects we don't know, we receive it but it is difficult because we didn't plan it … This is one of the weaknesses of the lack of joint planning. We have not yet identified the location to place the infrastructure – is it to be on private land? State land? Even if it is state land, someone might live there. How can we use the land? We have to negotiate, use our force, evict people from the land.[12]

While it is commonly presumed that the *suku* council will play a central role in managing these community issues, very often they are also at a loss as they were insufficiently involved in the project planning and unable to contain the tensions that external investment brings.

But there are also pockets of success in which particular programmes have made a positive influence. One of these success stories is in the rural water supply programme, in which community water management groups play a key role – and the key to their success is that they pay attention to *process*, endeavouring to shape the programme according to the community's structures and needs. When I spoke to various officials about the success of the programme, the common reply was that they actively engage across different sectors of the community, including various *xefes* and members of the *suku* council, owners of the land, *lia-na'in*, and various other community members. As they described it, the engagement is long term and planning is extensive, ensuring that people agree to take on responsibility for maintenance once the infrastructure is built (The Asia Foundation 2012a, 45).

The lesson is fairly clear: process matters, and the capacity to flexibly respond to the needs of different sectors of the community matters. As the director of one district-based NGO put it, 'Many times plans are made according to donors' desires. Because of this, development does not go ahead ... there is no sustainability'.[13] According to him, this approach needs to be turned on its head, taking a bottom-up approach which puts community needs first.

Conceptualising the *suku* council

As discussed in Chapter 4, the members on the *suku* council source much of their legitimacy by co-opting pre-existing customary relationships and institutions, and reinterpreting them into the new, state-based structure of the *suku* council. In the context of limited state resources and 'presence', this is how the council functions. However, in creating the *suku* council as a state-based, democratically elected body, there appears to be a common expectation that the council will behave as one would expect a 'modern' community representative body to behave – including sharing information and power within the council, and providing for broader representation in the *suku*. Because of the complexity of local governance, fieldwork has demonstrated that this has not always played out in practice. These weaknesses were recognised by one community member in Venilale, who explained:

> I think *suku* council is potentially a good governance body. Because if we talk about democracy and controlling power, that's one of the bodies that can share power and they can also control power of *xefe suku*. I think that's one of the things the *suku* council should be doing ... Not really concentrating on the *xefe suku* because the *xefe suku* can't do everything. So on *suku* council they have an expert on *lia-na'in*. They have an expert on youth problems. They have someone focusing more on women's issues. And the *suku* council can also give inputs to the *xefe suku*, right? But I don't think they use that opportunity ...[14]

The failure of many *suku* councils to share information and power in this way is often blamed on a lack of 'capacity', with different, well-intentioned NGO and government programmes aiming to address this gap. Such capacity development programmes can be useful, particularly if they are established on a long-term basis, by improving the motivation levels and capacities of individual *xefe suku* and other council members, which can vary significantly. But as a broader descriptor of local governance, such assessments of capacity need to be nuanced by also asking what norms of governance the *xefe suku* is following, and what community or other needs he is responding to. While *xefe suku* may not share much information and power with the council, they often do share information and power with other important, non-elected leaders in the *suku*. As the same community member noted, this comes back to the pace and process of change and the place of customary authority in the *suku*:

> As we know the experience of every country in the world, the more it goes towards modernity, traditions change. Traditional leadership will go to the side. But right now for whatever reason we keep it. For example, people like myself, I can say that traditional leadership is not good. But if we disrespect these guys in the community here, then we destroy a lot of things. For now, okay, this is the way of life in Timor. If we ignore it, we ignore our way of life ... That is why I say, let them rule, until they stop. This generation will move on.[15]

Beyond questions of capacity, this throws the spotlight on important paradigmatic differences upheld by customary governance, the pace of change in the villages, and the new expectations that are placed on the *suku* council. While the *suku* council appears to be well-established in the villages, varying from one *suku* to the next, it should not be forgotten that what makes it relatively functional as an organisation are the customary relationships which underlie it. This means that the tasks that tend to be easiest to perform are those which are based on the pre-existing norms of customary governance, as they follow well-worn paths that the community is accustomed to seeing their leaders carrying out. However, it becomes more difficult when the tasks involve a departure from customary governance – and it is here that we note the relative fragility of the *suku* council.

This fragility is particularly apparent when new, external resources are introduced to the *suku*. When we reflect on the 'inward-facing' nature of customary governance, customary institutions that guide economic relationships were never intended to guide the distribution of resources from external sources that enter at the *suku* level of governance. Instead, they are generally focused on social and economic relationships that bind the smaller family groups together. Because of its dependence on customary relationships and governance, the state-based institution of the *suku* council is also unable to easily contain new challenges that emerge when these limited resources enter the village.

In this context, the *suku* council can be understood as representing a thin 'layer' of state-based governance, which floats over the top of pre-existing customary governance norms, understandings of legitimacy and modes of accountability. While the *suku* council may be democratically elected with the mandate to represent the *suku* as a whole, the council is nonetheless comprised of individuals who ultimately see themselves as a member of their community – their *aldeia* and family group. Regardless of whether they are *xefe suku*, or *xefe aldeia*, or another member of the *suku* council, their sense of place, their source of wellbeing, and ultimately their sense of loyalty, always brings them back to their customary community.

Notes

1 Personal interview with *xefe suku*, 5 November 2008, *suku* Bado Ho'o, subdistrict Venilale (district Baucau).
2 Personal communication with civil society representative, June 2014, Dili.
3 Personal interview with *xefe suku*, 26 August 2008, *suku* Baha Mori, subdistrict Venilale (district Baucau).
4 Personal interview with leader of local NGO 'Esperansa', 15 January 2009, subdistrict Ainaro (district Ainaro).
5 Personal interview with parish nun, 8 October 2008, subdistrict Venilale (district Baucau).
6 Personal interview with domestic violence victim, April 2012, conducted through a consultancy with The Asia Foundation. Published in Asia Foundation (2012b, 8).
7 Personal interview with community member, 20 October 2008, *suku* Fatulia, subdistrict Venilale (district Baucau).
8 Personal interview with *lia-na'in*, 20 October 2008, *suku* Fatulia, subdistrict Venilale (district Baucau).
9 Personal interview with *xefe suku*, 9 January 2009, *suku* Cassa, subdistrict Ainaro (district Ainaro).
10 Personal interview with *xefe aldeia*, 28 October 2008, *suku* Fatulia, subdistrict Venilale (district Baucau).
11 Personal interview with *xefe suku*, 5 November 2008, *suku* Bado Ho'o, subdistrict Venilale (district Baucau).
12 Personal interview with district administrator, May 2012, conducted through a consultancy with The Asia Foundation. Published in Asia Foundation (2012a, 27).
13 Personal interview with leader of local NGO CDC, 15 June 2010, district Baucau.
14 Personal interview with community member, 14 September 2008, *suku* Uato Haco, subdistrict Venilale (district Baucau).
15 Personal interview with community member, 14 September 2008, *suku* Uato Haco, subdistrict Venilale (district Baucau).

References

The Asia Foundation 2012a. *Community Experiences of Decentralised Development*, Asia Foundation, Dili.
The Asia Foundation 2012b. *'Ami Sei Vitima Beibeik': Looking to the Needs of Domestic Violence Victims*, Asia Foundation, Dili.
Fitzpatrick, D., McWilliam, A. and Barnes, S. 2012. *Property and Social Resilience in Times of Conflict: Land, Custom and Law in East Timor*, Ashgate, Farnham.
Fundasaun Mahein 2012. 'Naktuka Incidents-Oecusse: Negotiation and Solution?', Press Release 6 March 2012. Available at: www.fundasaunmahein.org/2013/03/06/insidenti-naktuka-%E2%80%93-oecusse-negosiasaun-no-solusaun/.

Grenfell, D., Walsh, M., Noronha, C.M., Holthouse, K. and Trembath, A. 2008. *Community Sustainability and Security in Timor-Leste: Sarelari and Nanu*, Oxfam Australia, Concern Worldwide and Globalism Research Centre, RMIT University, Melbourne.

McWilliam, A. 2005. 'Houses of Resistance in East Timor: Structuring Sociality in the New Nation', *Anthropological Forum*, vol. 15, pp. 27–44.

Schulte Nordholt, H.G. 1971. *The Political System of the Atoni of Timor*, Martinus Nijhoff Publishing, The Hague.

7 Clientelism and patronage

No account of local governance would be complete without also considering the impact of many other organisations and networks that are established at the district and subdistrict level, which alternately challenge and draw upon customary and state institutional forms in different ways. Communities that continue to live what many would consider a 'traditional' way of life do not operate in complete isolation from other influences in the state. Even people from very remote communities are aware of, and at least to some extent engaged in, the 'modern' aspects of the state: voting in regular elections, participating as members of a political party, possibly helping with Church or local non-governmental organisation (NGO) activities, and accommodating visits from the police and other representatives of the state. Community members' direct exposure to these influences varies, with some people limiting their engagement to collecting their government payments, or casting their vote in elections, and others more actively engaged in different groups, networks and organisations. While direct engagement with the state varies significantly from one person to the next, there are changes that have been taking place at a broader systemic level, as ideas of liberal democracy take hold, and the market economy opens up. These new influences work in sometimes quite powerful ways to transform communities as new ideologies take root, and investment from the government or NGOs works to strengthen the influence of the capitalist monetary economy in what was previously a subsistence agricultural community. All of these changes work to render local governance more complicated, opening up new challenges and opportunities for community members and those who engage with them.

As we have already explored, while the *suku* council as a state-based organisation may in some ways be considered proof of the government's penetration and influence within the villages, the reality is far more complex. For the *suku* council, the current reliance on customary relationships and governance means that there are some things that they are well-equipped to do, and others that are more difficult – which is particularly the fragility of local governance arrangements in effectively and legitimately managing resources invested by external stakeholders. The importance of customary relationships, and the *suku* council's lack of legal capacity to manage government investment in the villages, means that council members, while elected, do not themselves represent the government. They are understood, both locally and legally, as community representatives, and as such trace most of their legitimacy to how well they are understood to represent the community (The Asia Foundation 2013). But nonetheless, they do perform many 'government-like' functions, and act as an important bridge for external stakeholders wanting to engage with the community. The balance that is found between customary and state-based governance as local authorities carry out their work varies from one village to the next, and also changes over time.

In terms of the formal government structure, the subdistrict administration is the most localised level of government,[1] housing various officials including the subdistrict administrator, community development officer, subdistrict finance officer, and others. It is up to the subdistrict administration to represent the government's interests and implement various programmes in communities. The subdistrict administration holds a central place in coordinating government and other activities, disbursing social payments to the elderly, widows and orphans, coordinating with different government line ministries and civil society on the provision of essential or emergency services, collecting and collating information, liaising with the district administration, working cooperatively with the police to promote security in the subdistrict, coordinating and sometimes 'reminding' *xefe suku* of their responsibilities under the law, and many more besides. Their responsibilities are numerous and to carry them out they must work in tandem with the various *xefe suku* and other leaders at subdistrict level, including the police, customary authorities, the Church, NGO officials and others. In addition to the subdistrict administration, there are other government representatives from the different line ministries that implement various programmes to improve agriculture, health, education, water and sanitation, give support to more vulnerable members of the community, and provide various other services. In a sense, the subdistrict administration can be seen as providing a type of 'glue' holding the disparate programmes and sometimes recalcitrant *xefe suku* together, with the overall cohesiveness of subdistrict governance highly dependent on the capacity of individual subdistrict administrators to effectively network and respond to the many different issues that arise.

Some subdistricts are 'busier' than others, with the number of government and NGO programmes operating in the territory roughly correlating to their proximity to district centres. These subdistricts are busy precisely because they have more programmes that are intended to improve the community. However, this increased assistance also comes with its own challenges. Integration of the various activities in the subdistrict can be difficult, as the different programmes tend to operate according to their own rules. Sometimes the subdistrict administration has a role in deciding the specifics of programme implementation; more often they are a conduit for other external stakeholders, providing advice but without much decision-making power of their own.

Their implementation also varies. Sometimes services are provided to community members from the district or subdistrict centre, other times they are outreach services in which government representatives actively visit the different villages as a part of their work. It is not uncommon to find multiple programmes all providing the same thing – or, alternatively, important community needs not being met due to buck-passing, as confused programme officials claim particular activities to be the responsibility of 'the other programme'. Managing these dynamics is a real challenge to a centralist state, as government capacity becomes weaker and more diffuse the closer it gets to communities, and the sheer number of projects and specific details becomes overwhelming. As explored in the previous chapter, the capacity of different programmes to deliver to communities depends on how well they are reflective of community realities. But a strong focus on community can also come at a price to overall government coherence at the local level, as there is less attention paid to horizontal and vertical integration with other programmes.

In addition to government programmes, civil society also has an important place in communities, with the Catholic Church playing a central role. The impact of the Church on local communities and local governance cannot be under estimated, as they provide essential services including schools and health clinics. Depending on the Catholic order established in the parish and the particular needs of the communities they serve, they may also provide outreach services for the very poor, or activities targeted specifically to young people, or be more focused on social justice and reconciliation issues. Their importance does not stop at the practical level. The Catholic influence in Timorese communities is strong, reflecting in part the important role that it played in the Timorese struggle for independence (Kohen 1999), as well as the length of time that the Church has existed in Timor-Leste. The focus of early Portuguese colonisation is telling, as it was Church officials rather than secular colonial officials who first established themselves on Timorese soil. It was only later that an administrative post was established to mark the Portuguese colonial presence.

Over the centuries, the doctrines of the Church have been interwoven with *lisan* so that they operate together in relative harmony. As one important customary leader who is also a deacon of the Church explained to me, much of the symbology of *lisan* and the Church are compatible – for example, the importance of blood sacrifice, which figures in *lisan* as well as the Old Testament. As he put it, the Church simply opened a new way for the people to access *Maromak* (God): 'before the Church came to Timor, we accessed *Maromak* through the rocks and the trees; after they came, we could access *Maromak* through the Church'.[2] This coming together of *lisan* and Catholicism is clearly evident on All Soul's Day, one of the most important holidays in Timor-Leste, providing an opportunity for people to return as a family to their traditional lands and observe the Catholic Mass as well as visit their family grave sites to acknowledge and venerate their ancestors.

The important place of the Church in Timorese life means that there are certain functions that it can carry out more easily than other, secular organisations. While the conservative influence of the Church has perhaps been problematic in national politics, it is clear at the local level that many priests and nuns provide vital services. There are many good examples of Church-based community work, one of the best being a domestic violence shelter in the town of Suai which was established by the nuns and which I visited in 2012. I was particularly taken with an outreach programme that they ran, facilitating acceptance of domestic violence victims back into their communities either while they were waiting for their case to be heard in the courts, or after their case had been dealt with, indicating that they were able to do things that other secular shelters struggled with.

As explored in Chapter 5, the sometimes very cruel 'blame the victim' tone of village attitudes towards these vulnerable women and children is an unfortunate reality faced by domestic violence victims and those who support them, effectively preventing such reintegration programmes in many areas. For many other secular shelters, when women chose to return to their village, it was generally understood as a failure of the support service – that the women were returning to subject themselves to further violence and abuse. But this shelter seemed to be different, they were somehow able to work together with the local leadership and run a positive programme of reintegration. As the coordinator of the shelter explained:

> When we began the shelter, people thought we were gathering 'bad' women, prostitutes, because they could see that they did not have a husband ... [But] we slowly taught them that this was not the case, that our programme was to make women strong. Now they understand. In the past, teachers would not allow girls who had been sexually abused into their class because their names had been dirtied, but now they understand the situation and receive the girls.[3]

The risk of upsetting a delicate situation and breaking the trust the nuns had established with these families meant I could not speak directly with the women who had returned to their villages. But conversations with the nuns working in the shelter, and with the police and other members of local civil society who were part of the referral network that operated in this district, all indicated that this little piece of magic was due in no small part to the respect the people have for the Church.

There are many other examples of civil society and government engagement in communities. Some are overwhelmingly positive, others more of a mixed bag, and yet others have been accused of causing more harm than good. While the particulars of successful community programmes remain stubbornly context-specific, there are broad lessons that can be taken from them. The golden thread is that all of them, in different ways, manage to appropriately intersect with community understandings of local authority and governance. This does not mean that the programme structure mirrors community dynamics – indeed, this is often inappropriate if it leads to the reproduction of existing inequalities and vulnerabilities. But particularly at those points where the programme deviates from community norms, programme managers have successfully translated their work into community realities, bringing in different sectors of the community to ensure a broad 'buy-in' of stakeholders, and displaying sensitivity and flexibility in responding to any unintended side effects of their work.

In examining these success stories, we can come to a few basic conclusions. The capacity of the individuals working in the programme to interact sensitively with local leaders (including customary leaders) is important. Programme workers' understanding of different sectors of the community, their sensitivities and their needs, is important. And the long-term nature of the programme, taking the time to plan with the community and respond openly to their concerns and priorities, rather than simply throwing money at a problem, is important. When we compare these to other programmes in which money was spent too quickly, without the requisite understanding of community dynamics, the difference is clear: what all of these factors point to is the importance of *process*. Even (or especially) in such potentially explosive situations as reintegrating domestic violence victims, engaging with the more conservative members of the community and bringing on-side customary as well as state-based authorities, can mean all the difference between a programme's success and failure. Every conversation with community members about programmes that they appreciated and took part in emphasised the importance of open, two-way engagement, and respect for the community, their leaders, their culture and their way of life.

Other networks and influences

Contemporary approaches to development and state-building tend to focus on the more easily recognised organisations such as *suku* council, government bodies, NGOs, political parties, the Church and others. But beyond these important organisations, there are many other informal influences, groups, networks and social movements which also exist in communities. There are local groups that have been formed by external stakeholders to fill certain specified roles in the community, such as friendship committees, water management groups, seed groups, and others, which are relatively easy for outsiders to comprehend as they form part of a larger government or NGO programme. But there are also indigenously-formed groups that have come together in response to particular needs in that area. These groups and networks are not necessarily customary, although they might draw on customary notions of authority and legitimacy. But neither are they easily understood as state-based organisations; while the larger groups may have a formal organisational structure, the way in which they operate is more akin to a social movement than a formal organisation. Some have an overall positive impact on the community, helping to strengthen their internal resilience by making the best use of community resources and empowering villagers to express their political views, such as the district-wide agricultural land rights movement, *União Agricultores Ermera* (UNAER). Others are more destructive, such as the martial arts groups and extremist political groups that intimidate communities, imposing informal 'taxes' on villagers, and/or burning down people's homes and worse during times of political crisis. These groups and networks exist all over Timor-Leste, and varying from one place to the next, their influence on community dynamics can be considerable.

These groups and networks, while 'invisible' to the outsider, sometimes have much greater relevance to community members than the more readily-understood organisations. For example, UNAER is a movement that is spread across the district of Ermera, whose members have banded together to claim their rights to the very valuable land and coffee plantations that they and their ancestors worked, but which are also subject to title claims that were granted during Portuguese times and taken over by Indonesian business interests during occupation. It is comprised of many different people, including local and customary authorities as well as ordinary farmers and community members, and is supported by Timorese NGOs and academics. As the president of UNAER described, while a *xefe suku* may be popularly elected, his legitimacy with the community is highly dependent on whether he supports the movement.[4] It began initially as a land rights movement, and in the early days of independence the farmers physically fought off those who sought to (re)claim the land. Now, most fights are conducted through the legal system as particular cases are brought to the courts, or are negotiated between parties in an external settlement. Customary authorities have a strong role to play in the movement. During a conversation I had with the president of UNAER in 2011, he described a recent customary ceremony that had been conducted by a group of *lia-na'in* in the lead up to an important case, in which the spirits sent a sign, clearly demonstrating who the rightful owners were. This effectively stopped the court case in its tracks, scaring the other side into a settlement before it was decided in the courts.[5]

UNAER is well-organised, with a portion of the coffee income from the different farming groups going to fund these court cases. In addition, UNAER has developed a number of community cooperatives, investing in the machinery to roast and grind the beans to ensure better returns for the farmers, and developing various other programmes, including building houses for vulnerable families and providing scholarships for promising young people to attend the national university. While typically not well-funded, there are many other groups and networks in Timorese communities that work and gain influence by following principles such as those that guide UNAER – strategically drawing on existing ideologies and understandings in the community and looking for ways to meet people's needs. In this, they often have a much greater chance at success than many government and NGO programmes because they emerge from the communities themselves.

But not all community networks and groups have a positive impact on communities. There are also violent martial arts groups and other extremist political groups that operate in different areas, causing serious problems for communities. In one village, there was an extremist political group responsible for burning people's homes in 2007 following the national election; in another, two martial arts gangs had clashed two years prior, burning people's homes and continuing to impose informal 'taxes' on community members. The influence of these groups reached a peak in the 2006–2007 Crisis, as the violence which pitted those from the east against those from the west of the country quickly splintered into complex lines of conflict and allegiance with different political and martial arts groups (see for example Scambary 2009). There has not been such a violent outburst of national significance in Timor-Leste since this period, however many of these groups continue to exist in their respective communities, consolidating their power locally and causing problems for villagers. On occasion, their influence may also spill beyond the boundaries of the village, attracting official attention.

Examination of how these groups and networks operate shows that they share many characteristics with those more positive networks such as UNAER. Key to understanding these groups is to recognise that their membership is not all 'mad and bad'. They all exist and gain influence because they fill the very real needs of their members, often providing a sense of empowerment in a governance environment where most feel politically disconnected from the state, or providing protection from other violent groups in the same area, or perhaps providing money, food or accommodation that assist in their livelihoods and wellbeing.

Whether or not members of these groups receive long-term benefit from these violent associations is, of course, a complex question. But the felt empowerment of their members, at least in the beginning of their association, is very real – and is central to understanding how these groups operate. The relative ease with which different groups can attract new members came out clearly in a conversation I had with one young man in 2008, who had joined an extremist political group well-known for house-burnings across a subdistrict the year before. This young man came from a very distant village, the oldest child of a family that suffered greatly during the 'hungry season' – that period of time between the end of the last crop and the beginning of the new. He was illiterate and had never been to school. For employment, the best he could hope for was very sporadic security employment by local contractors. Although the group he had joined was connected to a political party, the factors that were most important to him had nothing to do with political ideology, relating instead to his need for respect and self-respect, and a sense of belonging and empowerment. To fill these needs, he was given military-style rank in the group. His initiation to the group was cemented by drinking blood to signify an unbreakable bond, thereby securing his allegiance to the group and willingness to be one of the 'soldiers' if his leaders called on him. He was well aware that once he took the decision to join the group, it would be very difficult for him to leave.

I tell this story not to demean the fact that all he needed was a rank in order to become an unofficial soldier – but rather to humanise him. During my time in Timor-Leste, I have met many young men like him, young men who are disenfranchised, who are poor and uneducated, seeing very little future for themselves and needing a sense of belonging. The violence and intimidation that they carry out on behalf of their leaders, against members of their own or other communities, is destructive. But their reasons are often heartbreakingly logical and basic.

The fragile links between the government and villages, and the potential for other political opportunists to fill the gaps, should not be under-estimated in post-conflict communities. Violent disputes within communities are often multi-faceted as underlying fracture lines are expressed in different ways, and can be inter-generational (see for example Chamberlain 2009; Gunter 2007; Rawski 2002). These conflicts may, and often do, link with national-level conflict; however, at the local level, they take on their own unique character as they are interpreted through local politics, which is then expressed through the more readily-understandable flash-points of political party affiliation, or pro-autonomy/pro-independence conflict, or affiliation to martial arts groups. This is not to say that people do not believe strongly in these affiliations – they do. Rather, the point is that as new influences and affiliations enter the community, these same groups will often gather around old fracture lines as they interpret the conflict through a new framework of affiliation and opposition, friend and foe. This legacy of violence, from which communities have not had the opportunity to fully recover, together with a feeling of being left behind as others reap the benefits of independence while they continue to live in poverty, create a fertile breeding ground for political opportunists who seek to use these groups for their own gain.

Local politics does not stop in the absence of formal institutional structures, and the place of common social patronage that underpins more formalised networks and groups provides an important backdrop for how local power structures are shaped. These dynamics are not limited to Timorese villages; similar problems have also been noted in other countries where there are inadequate linkages between the government and ordinary villagers (see for example Roberts 2009). In such situations, vulnerable people turn to more powerful people in their communities for help, providing the local political space for patron-client groups, and for political opportunists to gather followers and entrench their power in local communities (Migdal 1998; Sidel 2004).These networks and relationships are often neither state-based nor customary; rather, they tend to strategically engage with both in order to establish their power base. They exist by filling certain communal needs that the legitimate state-based or customary leaders are unable to give, by providing the social patronage which is so important to individuals who are marginalised from real access to the benefits of the state and the market economy (Scott 1972).

The different groups that emerge from common social patronage all vary in their function and form. They may draw on the very important relationships formed through the ex-combatants and clandestine 'brotherhood', or economic and political patron–client networks that often form an extension on the 'natural' communities of family groups bound together via *uma lisan*. Or they may include openly violent or intimidatory networks associated with different political parties, and martial arts groups. How they operate may also be quite different. They may appear fairly innocuous, for example the informal 'water committee' that controlled water distribution when I lived in Venilale, favouring families associated with the committee and effectively privatising this public resource by charging a fee of cigarettes or whiskey to other families in exchange for water distribution. As they provide an important community service by ensuring that the pipes are regularly mended and water is distributed during the dry season, this committee was generally supported by legitimate authority figures, such as the subdistrict administrator and elected *xefe suku*, who were under-resourced and over-extended. But it also supplies a source of income for the leaders of the group, through which they can cement the loyalty of other community members. Or the motives and outcomes may be much less innocuous, such as the martial arts groups in Ainaro who burnt down 50 houses in 2004 (Scambary 2006), or the martial arts group Bua Malus that was established in *suku* Fatulia in late 2008 and whose members were discovered 'taxing' various family groups within the *suku* (Radio TVTL 2010). Because these networks operate outside of recognised organisational structures, these dynamics are often invisible to external stakeholders. The leaders may be completely independent, or they may occupy an official position in the community which they can then leverage to provide for their informal network, depending on where he sees the greatest potential opportunity to pursue his own interest. While potentially quite dangerous figures in society, the impact that these leaders have is often not clearly seen by those outside the community, as their power and influence tends to only be visibly exercised over local communities.

A state-centred approach that places state-based institutions at the centre of analysis often misses these important dynamics completely. However, they are fundamentally important in communities, as the influence of these patron–client networks and the individuals who head them directly impact on people's lives. In the academic literature, individuals who successfully use such strategies to shore up sufficient power, enabling them to pursue their own interests outside of the state's control, are referred to as 'local strongmen'. They exist all across Southeast Asia and elsewhere, arising in what Migdal (1988) terms a 'weblike society' – a context in which social networks are stronger than state-based institutions – and often pose a challenge to customary and state-based governance alike. Successful local strongmen tend to have their own little 'fiefdoms' driven by social patronage, but as this is often not enough they also work across different networks to broaden their influence – including with national leaders, who, in turn, can call on these figures to help them pursue their own interests in the area. There is ample evidence that there are many such individuals in Timor-Leste, from the local to the national level, who can be called on by others during times of political crisis to mobilise their groups and cause problems (see for example Scambary 2009).

This was the case with one relatively minor local strongman in the village of Venilale, who I nicknamed 'the subdistrict cowboy'. This man seriously interested me. In the customary sphere, he was the head of his family, but nothing more. And while community members said he had stood for election as *xefe suku* 'many times', they also explained that they were afraid of him so he would never be voted in. He described himself as 'just a businessman'. Nonetheless, it was clear that he exercised considerable influence within the subdistrict. An important question therefore became: how could he gain such disproportionate influence outside of the institutional structures that people knew and recognised in the community? As the picture of how he fit into the local governance environment slowly came together, the answer was fairly simple: he was smart, he had money, and was an opportunistic networker. He headed up various formal and informal committees that operated in the subdistrict (which didn't require popular election), he was an important member of a local political party chapter, he had successfully established himself as an economic patron for various family groups, and he had strategically aligned himself with various customary and state-based authority figures. As one community member explained it:

> He has power because first of all he is part of Fretilin. Fretilin is a big party here, so it gives him that kind of influence. The other reason he has influence is because he is very close to the priests ... He works with them. The other thing he has in his favour is that he is a working man, he talks but he also works. Not like the others. So for me, in terms of when we talk about the dignity of human life, when we talk about respecting that, he is definitely not that kind of person. But he is a working man, he is part of Fretilin, he is very influential. He has access to money, and to people with positions in Dili. Plus, his brother who died in the resistance was an extremely important person in the resistance.[6]

Similar insights were shared in other interviews, and various *suku* council members spoke of his influence as they criticised his close working relationship with the *xefe suku*. He was very skilled at earning money, and then leveraging that money into different types of power in the village. As one *xefe aldeia* cynically put it, 'wherever there is money, he will be there'.[7] As fieldwork progressed, new pieces of the puzzle emerged as his influence as a local moneylender, and his effective control over shared resources such as water through the informal Venilale 'water committee' became apparent. He also worked closely with the priests and with the subdistrict administrator, assisting them with their various projects, who in an ironic turn of events relied on him to help them get things done, as they were under-resourced and over-extended.

His influence spread across both state and customary institutional spheres. When I spoke to the local *liurai* requesting an interview, he said that he needed first to request permission from the *datu* in the *suku* – and that this local strongman would be the person responsible for gathering the *datu* together for a meeting. As a result, this interview never came about. He had a certain ruthless practicality – I once saw him drag a young man out of his house by his hair because he didn't turn up to a meeting on time – and there were many whispers about him. Outside of formal interviews, people spoke of his and others' responsibility for the political violence the year before. But he was helpful in getting things done, and unlike most legitimate local leaders he had access to real resources. Particularly in a local governance environment which is characterised by scarcity, power and resources are closely linked.

When we examine how he was able to gain such influence, his methods are recognisable: just as other authority figures strategically engaged across both state-based and customary institutions as they worked to fill communal needs and pursue their political agendas, so too did the local strongman. But unlike them, he made himself indispensable by specifically using the institutional 'gaps' where customary governance is no longer applicable but state institutional structures are fragile. His influence was never complete and there was a balance of power that was maintained as legitimate authorities also asserted their own positions.

Whether positive or negative, there are common strategies through which these more amorphous groups and networks establish themselves. And on their own, the dynamics underpinning these networks are neither intrinsically 'good' nor 'bad'. But they are, by definition, forces that largely operate outside of the state's institutional control. They can be fairly neutral or positive influences, such as unions, political parties, the Church or others, who all fill in vital gaps. But they may also be less reputable individuals and networks who are looking to shore up power for their own use, potentially running counter to the state's broader aims of promoting human security and protection of human rights. Working as he does outside a formal position of authority, how a local strongman uses his power is ultimately up to him, which can have serious negative impacts on the community as resources intended for the good of all are captured or diverted, and as his political interests are further pursued. Very often, the price that is paid is limited to those within the community. But in the context of limited state penetration and high levels of rural poverty, there is also a price that is paid by the state as the government has very little control over how the population's needs are met – or in who meets those needs. Over the long term, this can result in a state apparatus that appears strong but is actually quite fragile, which has important implications for how the government endeavours to extend its reach into the rural areas.

Looking for institutional 'fixes'

As has already been noted, the mainstream approach to development and institution-building tends to focus primarily on how 'strong' or 'weak' a state institution is. If state-sanctioned institutions or organisations are not effectively guiding community members to behave in certain ways, thereby working to shape the community more generally, this means that the institution or organisation needs to be strengthened. There may be a call for new laws or policies to be written. Or it may be thought that broad 'capacity development' is needed to teach relevant officials how to do their jobs better. Or there might be a restructuring of the organisation, or a reallocation of the resources available. The idea is that with appropriately targeted 'strengthening', these institutions and organisations will be able to 'contain' these other more negative influences that exist outside the state's control. What this one-sided logic fails to recognise, however, is that when they are introduced to communities, state-sanctioned institutions and organisations automatically become a part of the local governance environment. There is a mutual shaping at play: just as state-based institutions and organisations may influence individual and community behaviour, they are equally *impacted by* customary governance and other networks of influence. The development industry's insistence on focusing on clearly-recognisable organisational forms, to the exclusion of these other networks of influence, means that they often miss the real action.

As has been made evident, patron–client networks and local strongmen flourish in an environment in which the links between government and citizenry are weak, often resulting in lower levels of investment in the rural areas, or, alternatively, in investment that does not respond appropriately to community realities and needs. This represents a real challenge for the Timorese government. The presence of these other social forces and networks, through which much of the real political action in Timor-Leste takes place, has led to the seemingly paradoxical situation in which the state's influence through the *suku* council and other government bodies is undermined by a lack of state resourcing and 'presence' – but increasing rural investment is fraught in part because local institutions are too fragile to contain the potential conflict that may be sparked in the villages, and because of the risk that local strongmen will capture these important resources and institutions. This is the political context in which the Timorese government is now working to broaden its rural presence, through rural development programmes, and on a potentially much larger scale, as it works to fulfil its constitutional commitment to implement decentralisation.[8]

Decentralisation is commonly seen as a way to encourage grassroots democracy (Desai and Imrie 1998; Mohan and Stokke 2000), and is encouraged by various international organisations (including the United Nations (UN)) as an important 'fix' for states with functional institutions, but limited social legitimacy (Lemay-Hebert 2012, 476). It involves the creation of representative bodies that carry out important government functions at subnational levels of governance, with the general idea that these bodies will be better able to attend to the needs of the citizenry. However, while it is assumed that there is a natural link between bringing decision-making closer to the people and higher standards of government accountability, numerous studies indicate that this connection is

126 *Clientelism and patronage*

by no means clear (Mohan and Stokke 2000). As Daniel O'Dwyer and Connor Ziblatt note, 'in economically underdeveloped countries ... decentralisation actually is associated with *poorer* quality governance' (2006, 327). The democratising impact of decentralisation cannot simply be assumed.

In the Timorese context, the constitutional commitment to decentralisation is motivated by two major factors: the reality that the majority of the population continues to live in the rural areas, and the desire when the constitution was written to bring decision-making closer to the people (da Costa Guterres 2006, 234). Since the Local Government Options Study (LGOS) was conducted by the government of Timor-Leste in 2004, numerous legal and policy models have been put forward, each reflecting different approaches to what 'shape' decentralisation should take (RDTL 2004). Each iteration has dealt in different ways with the important issues of at what level of governance the representative bodies should be formed, how they should be structured, and how much power should be granted to them. Since the LGOS was first conducted, there have been intense negotiations around the questions over how power and resources are to be shared with the central government, as both the willingness of centralised ministries to share or devolve power, and the capacity of decentralised bodies to carry out their governing functions, have been called into question. Under the current model it is proposed that 13 Municipalities will be created, each of which are to be based in the current district centres, with the territorial borders to be broadly reflective of existing district boundaries. Representatives on the Municipal Assembly are to be popularly elected, and it is envisaged that *suku* council representatives will be able to 'provide advice' to the relevant decision-makers, but beyond this it appears their role will be fairly limited. It is yet to be seen whether this is the model that will ultimately be adopted in Timor-Leste, or if we see new policy models put forward in the coming years.

While it is clear that the implementation of decentralisation will involve major changes to subnational governance, it is less clear as to what those changes will bring. As noted previously, the logic which presumes that institutional 'fixes' can lead to predictable societal outcomes fails to reflect the mutual shaping that takes place, in which broader societal dynamics can also work to structure how the institutions work in communities. A major problem noted in other countries where decentralisation has been implemented, including Indonesia and the Philippines, has been the rise of clientelistic forms of governance, in which the decentralised institutions have been captured by political opportunists, who are then able to use the state resources to their advantage (Nordholt 2004, 45–48; Sidel 2004). Various commentators have noted the danger that similar dynamics might also play out in a decentralised Timor-Leste (see for example Kingsbury 2010, 33–34; Shoesmith 2010, 5).

Concerns such as these throw the spotlight on those important dynamics, groups and networks that most of the time remain 'invisible' to the policymaker, but which can work in powerful ways to shape whether or not institutional 'fixes' will be successful in meeting their policy aims. This points to the basic fact that legal and policy reforms by themselves do not create social change. Social change comes when these institutions are introduced to communities, who also respond in powerful ways to (re)shape these institutions to their liking – and that shaping or reshaping may run in the opposite direction to the original policy purpose. And because these dynamics are largely invisible to the policy-maker who is accustomed to working through the lens of state institutions, what anthropologist James Scott (1998) refers to as 'seeing like the state', policy-makers find themselves largely unable to anticipate where important policy reforms will lead them. But these results are not random.

These considerations bring us back to the important issue of accountability in governance, and to consider in more detail a particular version of accountability. As political scientist and former UN Senior Advisor to the Timorese President, Rui Feijo, points out, there are three distinct models for decentralisation, with each having different approaches to how power is shared between central and decentralised government bodies, and with each requiring different approaches to accountability.[9] Deconcentration is a fairly weak version of decentralisation, in which responsibility for certain services is transferred to decentralised bodies but with no real authority given to them. Delegation involves transferring authority and responsibility, but continuing accountability back to the central government. These two both involve a type of 'upwards' accountability, in which the decentralised body is ultimately accountable to the central government. The third model, devolution, refers instead to authority and responsibility being transferred to decentralised bodies, with accountability firmly tied to the citizens who elected them – emphasising 'downwards accountability', which can also be considered a type of self-government (Litvak et al. 1998, 4–6).

When we consider the different models for decentralisation, there are certainly clear implications for the quality of democracy that they promote. Democratisation theorists strongly argue that the accountability of decision-makers to the general population (i.e. downwards accountability) is central to a functioning democracy. From their perspective, downwards accountability does not need to be argued for because it is considered already to be a public good: if one is committed to a real democracy, one must also put measures in place to protect and promote accountability. But as has also been noted in the broader discussion on democratisation and good governance, when these ideas are put into practice, the focus quickly gets narrowed down to a much thinner version which focuses primarily on popular elections. Following this approach, it is thought that once the electoral apparatus is set up, we can tick this accountability box, content in the knowledge that the basic requirements for a democracy have been satisfied. The prevalence of this approach is not surprising, as the more substantive elements of democratisation are much more difficult to encourage, they take longer, they are hard to measure, and they are context-specific. There is no rule-book for implementing substantive democratisation.

However, the conflation of elections with democracy means that the administrative elements of governance – the important decisions that are made

128 *Clientelism and patronage*

between elections – are guided by other rules and policies that set up how the governing body should do its work. In the context of a decentralised polity, this tends to drag administrative attention back to issues of upwards accountability, as the central government endeavours to exercise important oversight functions such as ensuring effective service delivery and financial accountability. Nonetheless, as explored in different ways throughout this book, the tendency of public officials to 'see like the state' means, in the main, that they do not recognise, and are unable to respond to, influences that are of basic importance to community members. This means that they may also miss elements that are of vital importance beyond individual communities, such as (potentially) the emergence and capture of state institutions by local strongmen.

This is why community voices are so important. Community members do not see like the state; they see like community members. This is what makes a focus on downwards accountability, and efforts to bridge the gap between government and communities, fundamental to the overall aims of state-building and democratisation. What may be invisible to outsiders is often clearly apparent from the perspective of community members, and the more potential there is for open, two-way communication between villagers and decision-making bodies, the more likely it is that these important dynamics will become visible to all. This, however, requires more than the creation of institutional 'fixes' – important though these may be. It requires a broader, more creative look at how to build the necessary cultural-political linkages between villagers (who operate according to their own culture and worldview) and the government that represents them.

Notes

1 This will likely change in the future, as there are various policy initiatives in the pipeline that will involve significant government restructuring, including decentralisation and further regulations for the *suku* council.
2 Personal interview with *liurai mutin*, 17 December 2008, subdistrict Ainaro (district Ainaro).
3 Personal interview with coordinator of Uma Mahon Salele, Suai, April 2012, conducted through a consultancy with The Asia Foundation. Published in Asia Foundation (2012, 9).
4 Personal interview with UNAER President, July 2011, *suku* Ponilala, subdistrict Ermera (district Ermera), conducted through a research project for the Berghof Foundation (chief investigators Volker Boege, Anne Brown and Louise Moe, University of Queensland).
5 Personal interview with UNAER President, July 2011, *suku* Ponilala, subdistrict Ermera (district Ermera), conducted through a research project for the Berghof Foundation (chief investigators Volker Boege, Anne Brown and Louise Moe, University of Queensland).
6 Personal interview with community member, 14 September 2008, *suku* Uato Haco, subdistrict Venilale (district Baucau).
7 Personal interview with *xefe aldeia*, 4 August 2008, *suku* Fatulia, subdistrict Venilale (district Baucau).
8 The constitutional basis for decentralisation is laid out in sections 5.1, 63.1, 71.1 and 72.1 of the constitution of the Democratic Republic of Timor-Leste.

9 My thanks to Rui Feijo for pointing out and sharing his writings on the crucial differences between these different models, and their implications for accountability.

References

The Asia Foundation 2012. *'Ami Sei Vitima Beibeik': Looking to the Needs of Domestic Violence Victims*, The Asia Foundation, Dili.

The Asia Foundation 2013. *Reflections on Law No. 3/2009: Community Leadership and Their Elections*, The Asia Foundation, Dili.

Chamberlain, E. 2009. *Rebellion, Defeat and Exile: The 1959 Uprising in East Timor*, Point Lonsdale, Australia.

da Costa Guterres, F. 2006. *Elites and Prospects of Democracy in East Timor*. PhD thesis published January 2006, Griffith University, Brisbane.

Desai, V. and Imrie, R. 1998. 'The New Managerialism in Local Governance: North-South Dimensions', *Third World Quarterly*, vol. 19, pp. 635–650.

Gunter, J. 2007. 'Communal Conflict in Viqueque and the "Charged" History of '59', *The Asia Pacific Journal of Anthropology*, vol. 8, pp. 27–44.

Kingsbury, D. (2010) 'Decentralisation and Democratic Engagement in Timor-Leste'. In Farram, S. (Ed.) *Locating Democracy: Representation, Elections and Governance in Timor-Leste*, Charles Darwin University, Darwin, pp. 33–41.

Kohen, A. 1999. *From the Place of the Dead: The Epic Struggles of Bishop Belo of East Timor*, St Martin's Press, New York.

Lemay-Herbert, N. 2012. 'Coerced Transitions in Timor-Leste and Kosovo: Managing Competing Objectives of Institutional Building and Local Empowerment', *Democratization*, vol. 19, no. 3, pp. 465–485.

Litvak, J., Ahmad, J. and Bird, R. 1998. *Rethinking Decentralization in Developing Countries*, The World Bank, Washington, DC.

Migdal, J.S. 1988. *Strong Societies and Weak States: State-Society Relations and State Capabilities in the Third World*, Princeton University Press, Princeton.

Mohan, G. and Stokke, K. 2000. 'Participatory Development and Empowerment: The Dangers of Localism', *Third World Quarterly*, vol. 21, pp. 247–268.

Nordholt, S. 2004. 'Decentralisation in Indonesia: Less State, More Democracy?' In Törnquist, O., Harriss, J. and Stokke, K. (Eds) *Politicising Democracy: The New Local Politics of Democratisation*, Palgrave Macmillan, Basingstoke, pp. 29–50.

O'Dwyer, C. and Ziblatt, D. 2006. 'Does Decentralization Make Governments More Efficient and Effective?', *Commonwealth and Comparative Politics*, vol. 44, no. 3, pp. 326–343.

Radio TVTL 2010. 'Bua Malus Group Members Allegedly Claiming Money from Venilale Residents', 22 February 2010, Dili, Timor-Leste.

Rawski, F. 2002. 'Truth-Seeking and Local Histories in East Timor', *Asia-Pacific Journal on Human Rights and the Law*, vol. 3, pp. 77–96.

RDTL 2004. *Local Government Options Study*, Ministry for State Administration, Dili, Timor-Leste.

Roberts, D. 2009. 'The Superficiality of State Building in Cambodia: Patronage and Clientelism as Enduring Forms of Politics'. In Paris, R. and Sisk, T. (Eds) *The Dilemmas of Statebuilding: Confronting the Contradictions of Postwar Peace Operations*, Routledge, London and New York, pp. 149–169.

Scambary, J. 2006. *A Survey of Gangs and Youth Groups in Dili, Timor-Leste*, AusAID, Dili, Timor-Leste.

Scambary, J. 2009. 'Anatomy of a Conflict: The 2006–2007 Communal Violence in East Timor', *Conflict, Security and Development*, vol. 9, pp. 265–288.

Scott, J. 1972. 'Patron-Client Politics and Political Change in Southeast Asia', *The American Political Science Review*, vol. 66, pp. 91–113.

Scott, J. 1998. *Seeing Like a State*, Yale University Press, New Haven.

Shoesmith, D. 2010. 'The Politics of Decentralisation in Timor-Leste: A Comparative Analysis'. In Farram, S. (Ed.) *Locating Democracy: Representation, Elections and Governance in Timor-Leste*, Charles Darwin University, Darwin, pp. 3–10.

Sidel, J.T. 2004. 'Bossism and Democracy in the Philippines, Thailand and Indonesia: Towards an Alternative Framework for the Study of "Local Strongmen"'. In Harriss, J., Stokke, K. and Törnquist, O. (Eds) *Politicising Democracy: The New Local Politics of Democratisation*, Palgrave Macmillan, Basingstoke, pp. 51–74.

8 Taking local politics seriously

We began this book by considering the international development industry's approach to state-building, and the institutionalist assumptions that underpin the notion that a state can simply be 'built' through the introduction of liberal democratic institutions. As has been explored from different angles throughout this book, this approach is largely based on a functional understanding of institutionalism that presumes that if we find the 'right' institutional mix – a complex task, but still not dissimilar to a mechanical problem – then society will 'develop'. Communities will be transformed in a predictable manner. Individuals' lives will be improved. This approach, however, fails to engage with the basic reality that institution-building and institutionalisation are fundamentally political processes, and cannot be separated from the society and cultural context in which they operate. To the contrary: just as institutions may work to influence dynamics in communities and broader societies, so too are institutions themselves shaped as they are interpreted, adapted and applied by communities and community members according to their own norms, values, needs and material realities (Brown 2009, 146).

When institutions or external resources are introduced into communities, these new influences automatically become part of the local political environment, to be promoted, ignored, used or subverted, as the case may be. Close examination of governance in Timorese villages demonstrates the fluidity of these arrangements as identities, norms and values are alternately reproduced and contested as an integral part of local politics. It is through this process of exchange, as villagers bring their own interpretations to the institutions according to their particular local context, that they are interpreted and acquire meaning within the community.

These fluid interactions all indicate a central point so often missed by the mainstream, top-down approach to development. In the villages, people are not merely *acted upon* by decisions made on high. They are active agents in their own lives, families, cultures and communities. They make logical decisions, based on the information that they have, and the resources they have to hand, that are intended to improve their lives, and the lives of family members and others who are close to them. Sometimes they draw on customary institutions and locally-available resources to do this; other times they draw on state-based institutions and resources from external stakeholders. Very often, they draw on a complex combination of both. Regardless, the central guiding feature is not a preoccupation with whether or not a proposed solution falls under the banner of 'customary' or 'state-based' governance. Rather, the determining factor is whether it will work. As with all communities across the globe, villagers look for solutions that will fill their needs (including spiritual needs) in a legitimate and effective manner. The process as they look to fill these needs is inherently messy, as local authorities and community members engage with each other, and political opportunists grab whatever comes their way. And the balance that is found between state-based and customary governance is different from one community to the next, meaning that the overall power dynamics often vary considerably between different villages.

As we have also seen, the interaction between customary and state-based governance is not always fair. The decisions of local authorities, which determine to a large extent how customary and state-based norms are balanced, can also mean that the interests of those who are most vulnerable are sacrificed for the communal good. This is the route through which existing inequalities relating to gender and class are reproduced through the institutions of the state. As they enter the local political environment, state-based institutions are interpreted and used in ways that are concordant with existing power relationships and customary modes of governing – but they nonetheless retain their quality as 'modern' state institutions, clearly distinguishable from customary governance. This dynamic can serve to both deepen and legitimise those inequalities within communities, sometimes even meaning that they work against their original policy intent. Such a dynamic can be seen, for example, in the experiences of many female victims of domestic violence, who find themselves trapped by a variety of forces, including the pressures of her and her husband's family to remain with her violent spouse; the approach of customary authorities that focus on repairing the family unit and avoiding future violence by changing *her* behaviour; her economic situation with no income of her own but many children to care for; and the limited options available to her if she goes to state authorities for help. For these women, they can find themselves being 'bounced' from one authority to the next as they seek help from the police, family patrons, customary authorities, and others. Dynamics such as these show that the introduction of institutions that may look good on paper, but which fail to engage with existing social practices and norms, will rarely bring results that resonate with communities and respond to their needs. Failure to recognise and engage with these realities can result in missed opportunities – or worse, subversion or capture by political opportunists who look to promote their own interests through these same institutions.

What has also been demonstrated is that the failures associated with mainstream approaches to institution-building do not always stop at the local level. Missed opportunities and unintended side effects of well-intentioned development efforts can also deepen divisions or inequalities within or between

Taking local politics seriously 133

communities, exacerbating old problems and creating new ones. This can be seen, for example, in the institutional gaps that have arisen and are now being filled by patron–client networks, and the local strongmen who work to consolidate their interests. These dynamics are often invisible to those outside the community, and so remain largely unrecognised unless their influence widens and they are labelled 'troublemakers'. When they finally do attract official attention, the conventional response to such troublemakers is to bring in the police or the military to deal with the immediate threat. Vague notions of 'culture' or 'ethnicity' are blamed by confused outsiders, and the incident is pointed to as 'proof' that the state needs further strengthening to contain the 'threat' that is posed by different clan identities. As has been explored, however, this focus ignores the other drivers of violence – in particular, the weak economic and political links between the government and citizens that make it relatively easy for local opportunists to gather a broad following and use them to pursue their own interests. The symptoms (the 'troublemakers') are dealt with, but there is no clear path forward in dealing with the underlying causes and building more resilient communities and inclusive linkages between the government and the broader population.

All of these points demand a more nuanced and, to repeat, humble approach to our expectations of what institutional interventions can and should bring, shifting attention from an idealised expectation of the institutional *outcomes* to recognising the importance of *process*. This in turn forces us to actively engage with communities and to learn through that process of engagement, instead of presuming a simplistic cause–effect relationship between institutions and societal outcomes. These lessons apply not only to engagement with individual communities, but are also central to understanding the broader impact of state-building in Timor-Leste, and elsewhere.

Bringing it back to the state

As we have explored, the development industry's general approach to state-building is largely pro forma, imposing a vision of 'the state' which has very little to do with existing identities, networks and relationships. However, this approach as it has been (and continues to be) applied in Timor-Leste also appears to have forced a price to be paid in the *quality* of democracy and citizenship.

This requires some explanation. It's not that the institutions themselves are right or wrong, good or bad, as the technical quality of the institutions obviously varies from one set of policies and laws to the next. Nor is this a comment on whether or not the institutions are considered necessary for the state to function; there is no question that there are many institutions that are required to keep the state machinery operational, economy working and vital services running. Rather, this point relates to the *process* of state-building as it has played out in Timor-Leste. By prioritising the technical elements of institution-building over encouraging real, popular participation, form was put before substance. The key elements that normally accompany political change when it occurs organically were put aside – meaning that the messy but necessary disagreements over conflicting visions and ideals, and articulation of state-building into people's lived experience, were missed. By using the money and power that is available to major agencies such as the United Nations (UN) and various donor agencies, institution-building was separated from these other important considerations. And the board was artificially tilted in favour of those who gained positions of power in government, without the political need to build up popular support for their vision of the nation.

It has already been noted that the current governance environment in Timor-Leste is characterised by a major 'gap' between the centralist government structure and the majority of the population who live in the rural areas. This gap was criticised as a key failure of United Nations Transitional Administration for East Timor (UNTAET) during the early days of state-building, as language and cultural barriers meant that the UN worked together with key Timorese leaders, but the majority of the population were not included and were in fact unclear on what was happening (Chopra 2003; Federer 2005; Hohe 2002). These early decisions set the scene for further state-building once the UN handed power to the newly-elected Timorese government in 2002. Since then, while there have been dramatic improvements in many areas of government, this gap between the government and communities has remained stubbornly resistant to change, with institutional 'fixes' such as various rural development programmes only playing at the edges of the problem – and sometimes also causing new issues to arise. The failure of these rural development programmes to address this gap comes back to the central fact that it is not only about money, although the significantly lower levels of development spending in the villages compared with the investments that have been made in the urban areas is the most commonly-noted dimension. A less obvious, but over the long term potentially more corrosive, dimension to this gap between decision-makers and ordinary citizens is the issue of cultural-political linkages that shape the quality of relationship between the government and its people.

Just as institutions cannot be separated from the political and social context in which they are being implemented, state-building cannot be divorced from these broader cultural-political connections without introducing a dysfunctional element to political relationships and modes of development. This is what appears to have occurred in the Timorese context, where there are weak links between decision-makers and the population that they represent. Contemporary approaches to development that focus on state institutions are poorly suited to dealing with these challenges. As we have explored, state-centric approaches not only fail to respond to important interactions that fall outside the legal and political field of reference that is considered important to the state, they can actually work to render these interactions *invisible* to the outsider. And yet, these are often the very interactions that are of most importance to community members. As a result, villagers live in what appears to be a completely different world to the one inhabited by decision-makers, and in which there are few opportunities for real, balanced dialogue that might bring them closer together. When we consider how local authority is gained and maintained, or the values that underlie local dispute resolution, or the economic mechanisms that bind communities together, it is clear that many of the relationships and worldviews that make local institutions relatively functional also tend to fall outside the field of reference considered 'relevant' to the state. The gap in investment between urban and rural areas is a symptom of this much wider disconnect.

This fundamental disconnect between government and local communities manifests in a variety of ways. It can be seen, for example, in the problem of dependency noted by many district government officials and non-governmental organisation (NGO) workers, who commonly bemoan that communities are unwilling to participate and contribute to local development projects unless they are paid – even if they are the intended beneficiaries. This is sometimes called the '$3 problem', in reference to the expectation originally set up by early UN projects that people would be paid a daily wage of $2 or $3 for local construction work. But it also describes the broader problem that many local leaders identify, in which they describe the waning 'spirit of volunteerism' that was once so important in their community, and which is now being replaced with an expectation that the government should provide for them. This mentality of dependency is a real concern for local development in the country, and is often used as proof by frustrated government workers that the local people are lazy and unwilling to improve their own lives. Seen from the perspective of community members, however, the issue takes a different tone, reflecting the weak relationship between the government and ordinary citizens. If it is believed that decisions are being made by 'Dili elites' with no real respect for their culture and way of life, and if it is thought that the real benefits of independence are only going to a select few, with little regard to ordinary people's lives, there is little surprise that local apathy, withdrawal and sometimes resistance are emerging.

The dysfunction which comes about because of the incapacity of the state to 'see' beyond its own institutions can also express itself in terms of a lack of real connection and sense of responsibility by policy officials to the communities they are working for. The Timorese state apparatus was set up, as bureaucracies are, to create and maintain state institutions. But for key decision-makers, this means there are few political incentives to invest in articulating these efforts into people's lived experience, because the specified 'outcomes' of attending to government institutions are more readily met through bureaucratic processes. And for most bureaucrats, there are few visible rewards to engage in real, open dialogue, as their overall performance is evaluated against how well they meet specified programme, policy or broader institutional objectives. These dynamics create a path dependency (see for example Pierson 2004) in which institutional and organisational needs continue to be served, but the gap between government and the rest of the population remains largely untouched.

It is difficult to see how the creation of more policies or laws can deal with these issues – particularly when we consider that the disconnect between the government and the population came about in no small way *because of* the artificial separation of institution-building from other important dimensions of state-building. As we have explored, one political response put forward, and also written into the Timor-Leste constitution, is for the government to implement decentralisation with the intent of bringing decision-making closer to the people. There is no doubt: it is important to get it right. Depending on the policy model that is ultimately implemented, political decentralisation is potentially a game-changing move, involving a significant re-ordering of state institutions and distribution of resources, devolving important decision-making powers to locally elected bodies. However, it is also important to recognise that this, too, may not be enough. Experiences in other countries suggest that such an institutional 'fix' – massive though it has the potential to be – may not be sufficient to bridge the gap between elected bodies and the citizenry. As Törnquist *et al.* suggest in their examination of the 'democratic deficit' they identify in Indonesia, the Philippines, and the Indian state of Kerala, just as important as decentralisation is the issue of democratic 'scaling up' from communities to representative bodies (2009, 198).

If decentralisation is not also complemented by other efforts to build up cultural-political linkages between government bodies and communities, there is a distinct possibility that the current centralist decision-making government will be replaced with multiple decentralised government bodies that may serve the government, but are still characterised by weak links with the everyday citizen. In addition, as we explored in the previous chapter, there is also the risk that the decentralised structure and resources that go with it may be captured, to the detriment of communities and the broader political aims of the Timorese state. The lesson to be gained here, if there is one, is not whether decentralisation is appropriate for Timor-Leste. It is constitutionally required, and is an internal political matter for the Timorese people. Rather, the point is that while decentralisation may create a massive 'jolt' to current governance arrangements, there is no guarantee that the jolt will bring the presumed democratic payoff by bringing the government and communities closer together, as is often presumed to be the case.

All of these points bring us back to the central argument that while institutional or investment 'fixes' may form part of a solution, they do not by themselves create functional political relationships. As one community member and contractor put it, the conversation itself needs to be broadened:

> So far, we never talk about 'what is Timorese identity', what are the things that can keep Timorese together ... Our leaders, they talk about money, they talk about development, they don't talk about the one thing that is so fundamental – what is it to be Timorese? We have not done that so far ... What is our culture, and what do we want it to be in the future? We never talk about that. I think money and development is important, but

showing what it is to be human, that is something more than money. I don't know, that is my opinion ...[1]

Such questions cannot be addressed by more institution-building. They are more basic than that, requiring a broader discourse in which issues around culture and worldview, identity and nationhood come to the fore. Taking such an approach requires focusing not only on institutions, but also on the political spaces *between* the institutions, considering what has been missed in the state-building process thus far: namely, nurturing open-ended engagement between government and communities which emphasises the many social and cultural factors that bind communities together. Quite beyond questions of building functioning state institutions, these basic issues cut to the core of what it means to have a functional democratic state, and are all fundamentally political in nature.

By shifting the broader discourse from focusing on institutional outcomes to considering processes of engagement, new questions are raised, which potentially lead to new forms of engagement. State-building 'experts' cannot claim any real role in addressing these questions, as they must be resolved through political dialogue by the Timorese themselves. Ironically, however, these are the self-same questions which must be addressed if state-building is to succeed in its specified aims.

Looking forward, looking back

Questions of statehood and nationhood – of identity, culture and the building of cultural-political linkages between the government and Timorese communities – cannot simply be addressed via technocratic means. Nonetheless, when we consider the impact of early UN state-building, coupled with the ongoing focus of donors on promoting technocratic approaches through the provision of aid, what we see is a diversion of attention away from these basic questions of cultural-political linkages. This has resulted in a path dependence so that within many parts of the Timorese bureaucracy, and with the technical support of various aid agencies, there now appears to be such focus on the making of laws, and such faith placed in the capacity of institutions to somehow 'fix' the problems that are identified as needing fixing, that there is a misconception that these form the basic building blocks for an inclusive democracy. However, this is not the case, and focus on institution-building to the detriment of cultural-political links between decision-makers and the population they are there to represent is further entrenching these imbalances. Ironically for a development industry that defines itself by its capacity to promote democratisation and development, this artificial separation of institution-building from the broader cultural-political dimensions of state-building appears to have actually worked *against* developing a deeper Timorese democracy.

In part, the state-building approach reflects an underlying confusion in existing understandings of state- and nation-building itself. There is a vast array of literature on state-building and nation-building, but the terminology itself is not settled, resulting in very different visions of political community. But a common theme that threads throughout most of the literature is that a single political community must somehow be 'created' through political interventions, in order to bring together the different communities into a broad national identity, thereby overcoming the 'risk' to the nation posed by disparate local identities. This approach, nevertheless, misses the basic point that the nation of Timor-Leste already exists, given its most powerful form of expression in the 1999 vote for independence. Timorese identity and nationhood is not something to be 'built'. As we have explored throughout this book, communities are bound together in ways that are distinctly Timorese – responding through customary means to the pressures of Portuguese colonisation and Indonesian occupation, and now the challenges of independence.

The issue, therefore, is not whether a national identity can be 'built' from disparate local identities, in pursuit of some idealised form of homogeneity. At issue is the capacity of the state, and state institutions, to 'see' customary institutions, and to appropriately intersect with them in such a way that it strengthens overall accountability in the state, enabling people to participate as citizens rather than being shut out of political life. Regardless of the terminology used, what is often missed in higher-level discussions of state- and nation-building is that states are populated by people. And people live in their communities, according to their own cultures, modes of authority, relationships and networks. Any discussion that reduces state-building to the mechanistic 'building' of institutions automatically fails to recognise the importance of these other forms of governance, identities and relationships.

A shift in focus is needed. But this shift is not about 'romanticising' tradition. Rather, it's about bringing 'modernity' down from its theoretical pedestal and taking a more agnostic approach, looking at how people *actually* engage with each other, giving due weight to the underlying values (including cultural values) that inform their engagement, and considering what it all means for the future – the future of both Timor-Leste and of any other postcolonial nation hoping for the development industry to finally take their local politics seriously.

Note

1 Personal interview with community member, 14 September 2008, *suku* Uato Haco, subdistrict Venilale (district Baucau).

References

Brown, A. 2009. 'Security, Development and the Nation-building Agenda – East Timor', *Conflict, Security & Development*, vol. 9, no. 2, pp. 141–164.

Chopra, J. 2003. 'Building State Failure in East Timor', *Development and Change*, vol. 33, pp. 979–1000.

Federer, J. 2005. *The UN in East Timor: Building Timor Leste, A Fragile State*, Charles Darwin University Press, Darwin.

Hohe, T. 2002. 'Totem Polls: Indigenous Concepts and Free and Fair Elections in East Timor', *International Peacekeeping*, vol. 9, pp. 69–88.

Pierson, P. 2004. 'Positive Feedback and Path Dependence'. In *Politics in Time: History, Institutions, and Social Analysis*, Princeton University Press, New Jersey, pp. 17–53.

Törnquist, O., Tharakan, M., Chathukulam, J. and Quimpo, N. 2009. 'Popular Politics of Representation: New Lessons from the Pioneering Projects in Indonesia, Kerala, and the Philippines'. In Törnquist, O., Webster, N. and Stokke, K. (Eds) *Rethinking Popular Representation*, Palgrave Macmillan, New York, pp. 197–222.

Glossary

Aldeia Village
Barlake 'Bride price'; traditional institution establishing mutual obligations between families through marriage
Chefe d'Aldeia Portuguese spelling of Aldeia Chief (see xefe aldeia)
Chefe de Suco Portuguese spelling of Suku Chief (see xefe suku)
Concelho District, established during end of Portuguese colonisation
Datu Aristocrats; regional traditional leader below the level of the royal family
Ferik Female elder
Katuas Male elder
Lia-na'in Translates literally as owner of the words; holds ritual and judicial power in the community
Lisan Traditional law; ethical system encompassing a worldview that recognises still-sentient ancestors. Often referred to by the Malay/Indonesian term *adat*
Liurai King, or royalty; from Tetun 'lord of the land'
Lulik Sacred
Maromak God
Matan dook Witch doctor, or faith healer
Nahe biti (boot or ki'ik) A woven mat upon which people sit to discuss and resolve issues in the community. A *nahe biti boot* is a large mat, to resolve larger problems, and *nahe biti ki'ik* is a smaller mat for smaller problems
Posto Subdistrict established during end of Portuguese colonisation, sometimes still used to refer to subdistrict in independent Timor-Leste
Reino Kingdom
Suku Group of villages
Tarabandu Traditional prohibitions to regulate parts of communal life. Often used to regulate access to and use of shared natural resources
Uma kain Household, comprising extended family
Uma lisan Sacred house
Xefe aldeia Chief of village
Xefe suku Chief of suku

Index

accountability in governance 127–8
administrative boundaries 23–6
agricultural land rights movements 118–19
Alcantara, Cynthia Hewitt de 11
aldeia 23, 31–2, 45, 96, 97, 103–4; financial resources 106–8
Anjos, Virgilio dos 66
armed resistance movements 31–3 *see also* FALINTIL
Associação Popular Democrática Timorense (Apodeti) 27, 29
authorisation models of leadership 67, 68–9

barlake (bride-price) 19, 87, 100–1, 102, 103
Belo, Bishop 32
Boaventura, Dom 23
Bua Malus 122

capitação (head tax) 22
Carnation Revolution 27
Catholic Church and links with *lisan* 116; role in community 116–17; role in local reconciliation 84
CAVR 28
Chopra, Jarat 35, 36
civil violence *see* 'violensia sivil'
civil war 28–9
clandestine resistance structure 31–2, 35, 37
'climbing the ladder' hierarchy of local authority 80–4
CNRT *see* National Council of Timorese Resistance (CNRT)
co-incumbency models of leadership 67–8
colonisation, indirect rule 23–6

Commission for Reception, Truth and Reconciliation in Timor-Leste (CAVR) 28
Common Country Assessment Team 9
communities: civil society and government engagements 117–18; external ideological influences on 114; government disconnect with 134–6; impact of religion on 116–17; legacy of violence in 121; programme implementation and delivery in 116; rebuilding cultural-political linkages 136–8; reinterpreting policies for 131–2
community-driven development program (CEP) 35–6
Community Empowerment Program (CEP) 35–6
community structures 96–7
Constituent Assembly (CA) elections 36–8
corruption 82–3; in Indonesian administration 30; *xefe sukus* 107–8
Court of Appeal 63
Cox, Robert 56
Crisis, 2006–7 the 38, 120
customary authority: legitimacy of 68–9; loss of leadership rights 70; structures 63–5; teamwork with police 84–5
customary authority figures *see lia-na'-in*
customary economic relationships 99–110
customary governance 44; co-existence with state-based governance 51–9; flexibility of 69–70; inequities within 132; modern jurisprudential issues in 91–2; non-inclusion in state-building process 48; overlap of state-based authority with 66–70; strength of 26

customary institutional structures 43–4
customary law *see lisan*

datu (aristocracy) 19, 23, 64; pre-colonial governance 20
Davidson, Kathryn 19
decentralisation policies 125–7; challenges with implementation 38–9, 136; models for 126, 127
decolonisation process: facilitation of 26–9; impact on colonised countries 4–5; start of movements for 25
deconcentration model for decentralisation 127
Decree Law 5/2004 *Community Authorities* 54, 62
delegation model for decentralisation 127
democracy: co-existence with *lisan* 44–8, 51–2; concepts and processes of 48–52; contemporary attitudes towards 57; misinterpretations of 50–1; processes in villages 58–9
dependency theory 8
development *see* international development
devolution model for decentralisation 127
dispute resolution *see also* domestic violence: gendered nature of 74; hybrid forms of governance 53, 79; institutional links 85–6; limitations of customary authorities 85–9; limitations with domestic violence cases 86–7; procedural elements of 80–4; protective and preventative processes 92–4; role of customary authorities in cases 88–9
District Administrators (DAs) 35
District Field Officers (DFOs) 35
domestic violence *see also* 'violensia sivil': outreach services 117; customary inequalities relating to 90–1; limits of customary dispute resolution 86–7; perpetrated by mothers-in-law 100–1; protective and preventative processes 92–4; role of customary authorities in cases 88–9
downwards accountability for decentralisation 127, 128
Dunn, James 24, 28, 29
Dutch colonisation 18, 20

economic development and distribution problems within *suku* 106–8

education: barriers for women accessing 73; opportunities for children 26–7
ema reinu (commoners) 19, 20, 23–4
European Union (EU) 9

family patrons 99, 101–2
family policing 101
family relationships 99, 100
Farram, Stephen 21
Federer, Juan 34, 35
Feijo, Rui 127
Ferguson, James 6
Forças Armadas de Liberatação National de Timor Leste (FALINTIL) 31, 33, 35
Forman, S. 45
Frente Revolucionária de Timor-Leste Independence (FRETILIN) 27, 28, 29–30, 55; wins Constituent Assembly majority 37

Galanter, M. 8
good governance: normative, standardised approach problems 10–12; theoretical frameworks for 7–12
governance *see also* good governance; hybrid forms of governance; local governance: accountability 127; levels found in villages 81
government: disconnect with communities 134–6; engagement with civil society 117–18; building cultural-political linkages with communities 136–8
Grenfell, Damian 80, 97
Gusmão, Kay Rala 'Xanana' 37

Hicks, David 26
Hohe, Tanja 36, 37, 38
Huntington, Samuel 8
hybrid forms of governance 3–4; dispute resolution 79, 92–4; local leadership 66–70; practicalities of 12–13; processes of 14–15, 17–18; shadow side to 86–91

Indonesia: brutality against East Timorese 32–3; corruption 30; invasion of Timor-Leste 28–33; misinformation via propaganda 27–8; popular vote for independence from 32–3; resettlement centres 30; social engineering via transmigration programmes 30–1

institutional gaps, filled by patron-client and others 133
institutional links in dispute resolution processes 85–8
institutional theory 2, 43–4
institutionalisation 76–7; approaches to 52–7; fluidity of 56–7, 131; mainstream approach inadequacies 2; process of 56; successful adaptations to suit local 54–6
international development 9; need for bottom-up approach 110; good governance frameworks 8–12; impact of interventions on communities 96; the development industry 4–7; mainstream approaches 124–5, 131, 132–3; in postcolonial context 14–15; value of interventions 6–7, 58–9

Jenkins, Kate 11

Klibur Oan Timor Asuain (KOTA) 37

land conflict 106; tenure 99, 103
Latouche, Serge 8
Law 3/2009 *Community Leadership and Their Elections* 54, 62, 63
Law 7/2010 *Law Against Domestic Violence* 89
Law and Development approach 8
leadership hierarchies 80–4
Legislative Council 25–6
lia-na'-in 45, 63–4, 66, 69–70, 82; role in dispute resolution 80–1, 85, 89
liberal democracy 11, 49, 51
liberal theory 49
lisan 3, 12–14, 21, 49–50; adaptability of 17–18, 57; co-existence with democracy 44–8, 51–2; compatibility with Catholicism 116–17; dispute resolution forms 74, 80–9, 87–8; failure to protect women from domestic violence 89–90; importance of 44–7, 64–5, 97; legitimacy of 44–7, 70; limitations of 91–4
liurai 64; brutality against own people 23–4; contemporary role 64–5, 67; pre-colonial governance 18, 20; rebellions led by 22–3; proxy wars on behalf of Portuguese 20–1
liurai metan 64, 65
liurai mutin 64, 65
local authorities 66–70; hybrid models for 67–8

local governance: hybrid models 53–4, 76–7; impact of religion on 116
local government representatives 115
Local Government Options Study (LGOS) 126
local politics: political economy of 103–10; socio-political legitimacy of 56–8; uneven power base and resources 13
local strongmen 122–4, 125, 133
Locke, John 49

McWilliam, Andrew 31, 104
Maromak Oan (Child of God) 18, 21
marriage relationships 100 (*see also barlake*)
Merryman, J.H. 8
Migdal, J.S. 122
modernisation theorists 8
Moxham, Ben 36
Municipal Assemblies 126

National Consultative Council (NCC) 34
National Council (NC) 34
National Council of Timorese Resistance (CNRT) 34–6
networks and influences 118–24; extremist groups, 119–22; patron-client groups 121–3; positive groups 118–19
New Institutional Economics (NIE) 9
Non-Aligned Movement (NAM) 5
North, Douglass 9, 43

O'Dwyer, C. 126

Pakote Dezenvolvimentu Desentrilizadu (PDD) 108
Pakote Referendum 108
Partido Democratico (PD) 37
Partido Povo Timor (PPT) 37
Partido Social Democratica (PSD) 37
patron-client groups 121–3, 133; political economy of 125; rise of 126–7
Plowden, William 11
police: behaviour in domestic violence cases 89–90; cases taken to 82–4, 83; dispute resolution 85–6; level of intervention of 91; principles for taking on cases 88; teamwork with customary authorities 84–5
political-military violence (the Crisis 2006–7) *see also* Crisis, the 38, 120

political nepotism 82–3, 105–6; community perceptions of 108
political parties 37; affiliation in *suku* council 54–6; formation of new 27; impact of party-political violence 50–1
popular vote for independence, violence 32–3
Portuguese colonisation: 16th—19th century 20–4; 1912—1974, 24–6; class-based legal system 24–5; indirect rule 21–2, 23–4; rebellions against 22–3
pre-colonial governance 18–20
Programa Dezenvolvimentu Integradu Distrital (PDID) 108
Programa Dezenvolvimentu Lokál (PDL) 108
Programa Nasionál Dezenvolvimentu Suku (PNDS) 108

Ramos-Horta, President José 32, 34
religion and links with *lisan* 116–17
rural development programmes 108–10, 125; failure rates of 109, 134
rural water supply programmes 54, 109–10

Saldanha, João 26
Santa Cruz massacre 32
Scott, James 127
state-based governance 70, 111; co-existence with customary governance 3, 7, 11–14, 45, 51–9, 131–2
state-building: community networks and influences in 118–24; mainstream approach inadequacies 1–2, 132–8; postcolonial context 4
state-provided services and limitations in rural villages 13
student resistance movement 32, 37, 47; compatibility with Indonesian pro-democracy movement 47
subdistrict administrators 26, 115–16; role in land disputes 82
Suharto, President 32
suku 96; generational familial conflicts 106–7; levels of cohesion within 104; project management in segmented 104–10; segmented nature of 97–9, 103–4
suku communities: Portuguese colonisation 23; pre-colonial governance 20

suku council 13, 70–6; customary authority in 66–7; gender quotas 76–7; modernisation of 62–5; old and new institutional figures within 71; ongoing challenges with 39; *pakote* (package) system 63; political party affiliations 54–6; reliance on customary relationships in 111–12, 114–15; understanding processes 110–12; weaknesses within 110–11; women's representatives in 71; youth representatives 71
suku lia-na'in 62–3, 69–71; customary rules 67; mediation role in disputes 82

Tilman, Mateus 64
Toennies, Ferdinand 8
Topass conquerors 19, 20
Tornquist, O. 136
tradition and modernity 6, 11–12, 111
traditional house candidate model of leadership 67, 68
traditional law *see lisan*
Traube, Elizabeth 23
Trubek, D.M. 8
Tully, James 44

uma kain 82, 96, 98, 99, 103–4
uma lisan 80, 104; clandestine networks based on 32–3, 122; importance of 44–5, 88, 97; legitimacy of 64, 68–9, 75; self-governing social structure 19–20
UN Resolution 1272 establishing UNTAET 33
União Agricultores Ermera (UNAER) 118–19
União Democrática Timorense (UDT) 27, 28
United Nations CEDAW committee 71
United Nations General Assembly 5
United Nations Research Institute for Social Development (UNRISD) 11
United Nations Security Council 33
United Nations Transitional Administration for East Timor (UNTAET) 10, 33–8; approaches to local governance 34–6, 46, 134; end of administration 38; failures of 35, 45–6; organisation of major elections 36–8
upwards accountability for decentralisation 127, 128

villages *see also aldeia; suku*: infrastructure management in 104–5; structures of 97–9; subsistence economies 102–3; *sukus* that border Indonesia 98

violence *see also* domestic violence: in communities 33, 121; community network groups that incite 119–21; party-political 50–1; political-military (the Crisis of 2006/07) *see also* Crisis, the 38, 120; post-election 32–3

'violensia sivil,' 91–2

Weber, Max 8

women: as customary authorities 75–6, 77; dispute resolution barriers 74–5; domestic violence shelters for 117; education barriers 73; failures of *lisan* to protect 89–90; economic opportunities for 103; gendered division of labour 101–3; inequalities for domestic violence victims 132; limits of customary dispute resolution 86–7; political participation barriers 71–3; as *xefe suku* 68, 75

women's representative on *suku* council 71–3

World Bank 5, 10; Community Empowerment Program (CEP) 35–6, 66; good governance frameworks 9

xefe aldeia (chief of the a*ldeia*) 62, 98; customary rules 67; division of power with *xefe sukus* 107–8; mediation role in disputes 82

xefe suku (chief of the *suku*) 62, 68, 81; customary rules 67; reliance on *xefe aldeias* 98–9; division of power with *xefe aldeias* 107–8; external assistance for projects 105; females as 68, 75; mediation role in disputes 82

xefe uma kain 82, 107

youth representatives on *suku* council 71

Ziblatt, D. 126